BOOK ENDOR

"*The Power of Submission* is an enjoyabl a very needed message in an age and culture that is disgusted with the very idea of authority. This book covers a breadth of areas, and its broadness is a strength. I highly recommend it."

—J.P. Moreland, Distinguished Professor of Philosophy, Talbot School of Theology

"Christians labor in a culture radically disfigured by contempt for legitimate authority. Indeed, authority is largely ignored and its corollary, submission, despised. Believers themselves have not escaped culture's tarnish. Some having yielded to these influences adopt values and practices that exalt personal, individualistic power. John Tebay offers a timely corrective that brims with fresh wisdom and insights. Anchored solidly in Scripture, *The Power of Submission* points the way to renewed commitment to authentic application of biblical teaching."

—Dennis Dirks, Professor Emeritus and former Dean, Talbot School of Theology (Biola University)

"In this postmodern age that highlights personal freedom and relative truth, *The Power of Submission* represents an important discussion on the concept of authority. Long lost in current theological reflections is any clarity as to how divine authority applies to the contemporary church. In this work, John Tebay offers an articulate and thorough exposition of God's authority and how it works out in the trinity, the leadership of the church, marriages and households.

"Foundational to his discussion is an examination of God's authority and the subjection of His Son, which forms a model for all that follows and is an important insight often lacking in discussions of authority. This thought-provoking work will be a valuable tool for ministers and elders as they lead God's people in understanding His authority."

—Ray McCormick, PhD. and Professor Emeritus at Azusa Pacific University

"Having served in eldership with John Tebay for over a decade, I have observed firsthand the principles of biblical authority at work in the Church that are clearly expressed in *The Power of Submission*. Having a clear understanding of biblical authority is foundational for the Church to function as God has designed. I strongly recommend this resource to all followers of Jesus Christ.

—Michael T. Peters, Managing Partner,
Ronald Blue & Co, CPAs and Consultants

"After John trained our elders and staff on the biblical model of authority in the Church, we totally revamped our elder selection and training process, resulting in a much healthier leadership team. Roles, responsibilities, and relationships to each other, to paid and volunteer staff, and to the congregation were clarified. We learned how to listen to God together. We learned how to shepherd those whom God has placed in our trust. *The Power of Submission* is a 'must read' for all leaders in a church."

—Frank Sung, former Elder Board Chairman at Seacoast
Community Church in Encinitas, California

John did a teaching series for our Chinese congregation on authority as well as men's and women's roles in the Church and the family. His teaching helped us establish a clear church structure and elders team, which has strengthened our leadership and helped our church to keep growing in the right way. *The Power of Submission*, which is a gathering of John's shepherding wisdom over sixty years, is a great treasure to the Church. I'm sure that anyone who reads this book will benefit from it."

—Tiangang Qian, Lead Elder, Chinese Congregation of
Calvary Community Church of Brea in Brea, California

"Working with our elders, John really helped us understand the importance of authority and submission in spiritual leadership. Every elder should read this book."

—Bill Buchanan, Elder Board Chairman
at Seacoast Community Church in Encinitas, California

"*The Power of Submission* is not simply a theoretical attempt to solve one of the latest crises in the Church. It is a comprehensive collection of truths gathered over sixty years from a ministry living out what Scripture teaches on a very important issue. From the beginning of time, the enemy has targeted the concept of authority. It is no wonder there is resistance and confusion, both inside and outside the Church. *The Power of Submission* systematically lays out a biblical foundation to understand God and His intention for authority. Yes, my father wrote this book, but I can't imagine any church leadership that would not benefit from collectively going through *The Power of Submission*."

—David Tebay, Elder and Senior Pastor,
Calvary Community Church of Brea in Brea, California

"*The Power of Submission* provides a deep, biblical understanding on the principle of authority and captures a fundamental comprehension that can be applied across cultures and to every category of community. Our Chinese congregation positively benefited from integrating these principles into our lives. Well worth reading!"

—Rong Zhao, Elder, Chinese Congregation of
Calvary Community Church of Brea in Brea, California

"Since the fall, man's rebellious heart has sought to separate him from a loving Heavenly Father. God's antidote for man's rebellion is submission to His authority. Taken from God's Word, this book by my father clearly represents God's heart for us by defining His authority in our relationship with Him, our church life, our society, our work, our marriages, and our families. This is a much-needed handbook for life."

—John C. Tebay, Dean of Fine Arts, Fullerton College,
and Pastor of Worship and Music at First Evangelical
Free Church of Fullerton in Fullerton, California

THE
POWER
OF
Submission

A Biblical Exposition
of Godly Authority in the Trinity,
the World, the Family, and the Church

BY JOHN TEBAY

Scripture quotations taken from the New American Standard Bible® (NASB). Copyright © 1960, 1962, 1963, 1968, 1971, 1972, 1973, 1975, 1977, 1995 by the Lockman Foundation. Used by permission. www.Lockman.org.

Published by Turning Page Books

Editorial assistance by Mike Yorkey (www.mikeyorkey.com) and Jessica Snell.

Cover and interior design by Emily Morelli (emily@bluemusestudio.com)

To contact John Tebay, write him at jandgtebay@yahoo.com or call or text him at (714) 504-5091.

TABLE OF CONTENTS

*All Scripture references come from the
New American Standard Bible (NASB).*

INTRODUCTION

A small but vibrant Christ-centered church in a rural area of our country had just called a new pastor to come and be part of the eldership of the church.

The congregation had been led by a godly, loving man for many years and had developed a strong unity among the elders and within the congregation. As a church, they had established a powerful witness and influence for Jesus Christ in their community. In His sovereign purpose, God moved the original pastor into another ministry, which created a need for a new pastor to join with the elders to shepherd this healthy flock of God's people.

Within a short time after his arrival, this new pastor found himself at odds over a particular issue with several elders. He was convinced that his position was correct and led the church into a split that involved the elders and pitted the entire congregation against each other—even families. As I understood the situation, there was no moral, ethical, theological, or biblical content that created the division. The reason the church split had more to do with people's attitudes about the way they worked with each other, the process that entailed, and communication with the rest of the congregation.

This story is sad and discouraging for four important reasons:

1. As anyone could imagine, the witness of this Christian community was greatly compromised.

2. The pain and sorrow impacted all the families in this community with unknown continuing effects on the lives of them all.

3. The strength of unity in the fellowship was significantly weakened.

4. It was all unnecessary.

All of the people involved, including the new pastor, were foundationally good, God-loving members of the Body of Christ. My analysis of this division was that the new pastor did not understand the principle of plurality in the authority of the elders. He put too much weight on his own leadership and did not protect the unity of the eldership—nor submit himself as part of that plurality.

This story could be told with minor differences about thousands of churches and Christian ministries throughout the world. It has been my observation, over many years of ministry, that this confusion about authority is usually centered around the pastor. While the congregation well may live in its own confusion, the pastor is usually the one who fails to understand the importance of *his* submission to the authority of the eldership, of which he is a part. I have also learned that unless the pastor is clear about this biblical principle, he will not empower his elders to function in a godly plurality with him.

The reason I use this church as an example is because it's in the church that this principle of authority needs to be understood and applied as a foundation for all other categories of relationships and community. Or, said in another way, the principle of authority is crucial in every category of community. I've found that it's in many of these other areas that a confusion about and resistance to authority glaringly exists.

I would like to further this discussion with words from the preamble to our country's Declaration of Independence, which declares that all men are "endowed by their Creator with certain unalienable Rights, that among these are Life, Liberty, and the pursuit of Happiness." Allow me to focus on the word "liberty" for a moment.

It's my conviction that here in America and other areas of Western civilization, we have distorted this concept of liberty so greatly that it's destroying us instead of freeing us. In an excellent article he wrote for *Crisis* magazine, philosophy professor James Jacobs asserts, "The idea of liberty has come to be understood as a libertine autonomy which pursues unfettered individual expression as the sole goal of life."

Then Jacobs had this to say:

> Traditionally, the idea of right implied an objectively correct state of affairs wherein a human being behaves and is treated in a manner befitting that human nature. In contrast to this, modern philosophy has abolished the idea of a universal human nature. Thus, rights can no longer be defined according to these objective moral relations. In place of this objective foundation, rights now arise from mere subjective preferences, which are to be protected from any interference by others.

What Jacobs refers to now as "objective moral relations," evangelical theologian Francis Schaeffer referred to as "moral absolutes" and "the rule of law" forty years ago. Schaeffer predicted that if our culture lost those moral absolutes, we would be left with arbitrary preferences in determining truth in every walk of life—judicial, political, academic, educational, and in the media and social interactions. I think that most of us would agree that his predictions have come true today.

Barry Cooper, an English author, speaker, and church planter, wrote a fascinating article that appeared in *Christianity Today* in 2013. Entitled "Imprisoned by Choice," Cooper referred to the false god of options based on Elijah's call on Israel to stop "limping on the two divided opinions" (1 Kings 18:21 from the Emphasized

Bible). Cooper's thesis was that we worship the "god of options" so we don't have to commit ourselves to anyone or anything. He cited psychologist Barry Schwartz in his book *The Paradox of Choice* where Schwartz asserted "that as a culture we demand choice. We demand options. We imagine that more options mean more freedom. And most people think that limitless freedom must be a good option." Schwartz goes on to point out that this doesn't actually make us happy.

It's my conviction that choice becomes an addiction and really means "I want to do what I want to do whenever and however I want to do it." This availability of choice seems so plausible and so attractive because it allows us to do whatever we want without interference from anybody, especially God. When we refuse to submit to God's authority, however, we end up resisting and mostly refusing any authority.

J.P. Moreland, Distinguished Professor of Philosophy at the Talbot School of Theology, noted this:

> This enslaving confusion about liberty and freedom can be put quite simply: genuine freedom is actually the power to do what I ought—not the right to do what I want.
>
> To illustrate: consider watching pornography. The second notion of freedom implies I have a right to view pornography and no one should be able to judge or stop me. The former notion of freedom implies that I have the power to resist viewing pornography and even get to the point of not being tempted by it. This kind of freedom brings life. The right to do what I want can easily lead to addiction, enslavement and death. The power to do what I ought requires submission to truth and reality.

Some people have the power to do what they ought when it comes to playing the piano. But this power came at a price: regular practice and discipline in submission to the nature of what pianos are and how they work. This illustrates that once we get clear about what genuine freedom is, that freedom requires submission to truth and the nature of reality, most importantly, as revealed by God in His word.

But in a society "imprisoned by choice" and drunk with subjective preferences that eventually bring social and individual chaos, there will always be resistance to submission to authority.

One of the areas of resistance to authority is perpetually and graphically seen in child-rearing. The majority of parents today have bought into the narrative that insisting on a child's obedience is mean and uncaring. That narrative has been bolstered by academic studies from universities on child development. We are told by academicians that to insist on obedience from your child is interfering with his or her individuality.

Consequently, as parents, we are always asking our children—before they are ready to discern—what they want to eat, what they want to wear, where they want to go, if they want to go to bed, and even, in rare but increasing instances, do they want to be a boy or a girl. We are training them to be addicted to their own choices and getting their own way.

I will never forget an incident that occurred in a parking area of Bryce National Park in Utah some years ago. My wife, Grace, and I had just emerged from the canyon after hiking and were getting ready to get into our car. We noticed a father trying to reconcile his protection of an obviously expensive camera with his two- or three-year-old girl dragging the camera along on the pavement by its connecting cord. When he took the camera from her, she proceeded to scream and cry. After a brief moment, he handed his expensive camera back to her and raised his hands as if to say, "What am I supposed to do?"

He finally picked the little girl up with the camera in her hands and walked off to his car. As I watched the scene unfold, I asked myself, *What would keep a father from using common sense to not let his toddler be in charge of that situation?*

Perhaps an answer to my question can be found in a column by John Leo that appeared in *U. S. News & World Report.* He points out that one of the bad ideas to come out of the 1960s was the concept of children's liberation. This notion was lumped together with the idea that women and gays were oppressed minorities "in need of liberation."

Several legal thinkers, including a Yale law student named Hillary Rodham in the 1970s, expounded the view that children should be autonomous and protected from the patriarchy of the past. John Leo cited Kay Hymowitz, a fellow at the Manhattan Institute, who explained that these child-liberation ideas entered the mainstream at this time and hardened into a philosophy that she called "anti-culturalism"—the idea that socializing children and attempting to mold the character of the young is a wrongful use of power by the strong against the weak. Children, it was said, should develop independently of the prevailing culture and even in opposition to it. This idea was radical because it forbade what all cultures have assumed they must do: transmit cultural values from one generation to the next.

"Anti-culturalism . . . is the dominant ideology among child development experts, and it has filtered into the courts, into the schools, into the parenting magazines, into Hollywood, and into our kitchens and family rooms," said Hymowitz.

Leo then had this to say: "It boils down to the notion that children should be allowed to develop on their own; that parents and schools should stimulate and encourage but otherwise stay out of the way . . . Children are not to be raised, but simply allowed to grow up. This may be the natural result of a theory calling for parents to be moral and cultural bystanders in the lives of their children."

The effects of this dangerous sociological and anthropological position have become alarming in our homes and schools, and has been fueled by our universities, media, and academic elites. My further assessment is that this entire movement is driven by a distrust and hatred of authority.

For me, the worst thing about this disintegration of authority in the family and in our schools is that it's diametrically opposed to the plain and liberating teaching of God's Word—the Scriptures. Jesus said if anyone would come after Him, let him deny himself (or say no to himself), take up his cross (or die to self), and follow Him. Amazingly, Jesus not only taught us about the importance of obedience and submission to God's authority, but He Himself made it abundantly clear that He also was under that authority and found obedience to the will of His Father to be the path of joy and peace and complete fulfillment (John 4:27-34).

To help our children be prepared to follow Jesus, we need to train them to say no to their own way and yes to God's way. We need to help them understand that the path of obedience is the path of genuine freedom, joy, and fulfillment. This is the position of authority and care God has placed upon us as parents. Living for themselves and going their own way is the path of frustration, misery, darkness, and death (Proverbs 19:18; 23:13-14). God's Word teaches, and my own experience affirms, that when we—both children and adults—live for ourselves and go our own way, we are never satisfied.

Our control is never enough. Our selfishness is never satiated. Our rebellion is never fulfilled. And our autonomous way of living is impossible and unacceptable even in our permissive society. There is always some place, some time that we hit a wall and we're unable to have our own way. This makes us human beings furious and often results in horrendous, enraged violence and even death—as witnessed by the frequency of school and workplace shootings—which we experience all too regularly in our lost society.

* * *

Another key area in our culture where the principle of authority has been under attack for decades is our sexuality. The protest movement of the Sixties included a massive "sexual revolution." This development was powerfully connected to a movement to break down, distrust, and hate all authority. The commitment to total freedom as a "libertine autonomy which pursues unfettered individual expression"—as professor James Jacobs wrote—and as the highest and only goal in life, exploded like a dynamite charge that blew up most restraints and order about anything, especially sexuality.

It's my conviction that this philosophy of life has been driven by years of bowing down to academia's beloved icon of human behavior, Sigmund Freud, who taught that most of the mental and emotional problems found in humans were products of a too restrictive socialization in the family and society as a whole. Specifically, Freud declared, the repression of sexual desire resulted in fear, anxiety, and depression.

O. Hobart Mower, the late Research Professor of Psychology at the University of Illinois, published a scathing critique of Freud's theories entitled *The Crisis in Psychiatry and Religion* back in 1961. He pointed out that toward the end of the 19th century, "crowds of neurotics" hurried from one physician to another with their troubles. Mower continues the narrative by saying this:

The situation thus called for a boldness which Freud supplied . . . Guilt, he hypothesized, was indeed a factor in neurosis but it was a false, unrealistic, and crippling guilt which, as a result of a too strict and restricting socialization of the individual, impeded the normal flow of certain instinctual energies, notably those of sex and aggression. So the psychoanalytic physician set out to cure neurotic individuals by championing the rights of the body in opposition to a society and *moral order* [italics mine] which were presumed to be unduly harsh and arbitrary.

Mower cited David Bakan who, in his book, *Freud and the Jewish Mystical Tradition*, assembled powerful evidence that led him to believe that Freud not only repudiated Mosaic and Christian conceptions of God, but in addition, "identified himself with the Devil."

Bakan further explains by stating this: "Now what is the Devil, psychologically? The answer is eminently simple, on one level. The Devil is the suspended superego. He is the permissive superego. The Devil is that part of the person which permits him to violate the precepts of the superego."

Referring to Freud's theories of psychoanalysis, Mower writes:

We cannot at this point in time, regard his total effort as anything but a failure. In fact, this surely is the hallmark of Evil: ultimate disaster after what appears to be great accomplishment and gain. It is the long haul that provides the test of rightness and righteousness: and already, barely two decades after Freud's death, the signs of confusion and disintegration in the movement he launched are rampant.

E. Michael Jones in his book, *Degenerate Moderns: Modernity as Rationalized Sexual Misbehavior*, asserts that Freud's psychological theories were fueled by his illicit sexual relationship with Minna Bernays, his wife's sister. This he ties, based on numerous sources, to the apparent obsession that Freud had with incestual relationships and, according to Freud, men's desires to have sexual relations with their mothers or sisters. All of this goes to say that Freud's system of psychoanalysis was a product of his own confused and deviant sexuality.

What is crucial here is Freud's concept that the repressive, restrictive superego needs to be replaced by the *permissive superego* so people can be healed of their neuroses. A permissive superego defines the anti-authority, "anything goes" philosophy of life that dominates our universities, our media, our entertainment industry, our educational systems and, depending on who is in office, much of our body politic. The application of this anti-authority, sexual revolution has created complete chaos in our sexual understanding and behavior.

Consider what Miley Cyrus, a Disney performer in her earlier years, says about her sexuality these days. "I'm very open about it—I'm pansexual," she told *Yahoo News*. "But I'm not in a relationship. I'm 22, I'm going on dates, but I change my style every two weeks, let alone who I'm with." In another interview, she said, "I don't relate to being boy or girl, and I don't have to have my partner relate to boy or girl."

The underlying tragedy is that the Yahoo reporter acted as though this was a legitimate discussion about sexuality. I'm not bringing judgment upon Miley Cyrus but rather calling out a permissive society that glorifies "unfettered individual expression," which has come to mean the rejection and hatred of authority and any restraints it puts on our personal choices.

My heart breaks for Miley Cyrus and all who are confused about their sexual lifestyles in today's sex-obsessed culture. It's not just the deviant sexual lifestyles that give us pause, however. If we take our current TV shows, movies, and literature seriously, heterosexual activity apart from marriage is approved by a significant minority, if not a majority, in our American society. Men and women living together without benefit of matrimony is commonplace. Hook-up apps like Tinder or Badoo make it easy to seek out one-night stands. News stories of female teachers having sex with male high school students are alarmingly frequent. And recently Americans have watched the exposure of sexual harassment among media figures like Harvey Weinstein and Matt Lauer as well as a host of politicians, star athletes, and famous actors. It seems like every day there's a new revelation of sexual aggression and abuse by a man in a position of power.

We are paying the bill for the disintegration of our collective moral order, codified and effectively promoted by Freud. Underlying this chaotic and destructive sexual revolution is the repudiation of God's authority, when God Himself is the source of all authority.

All understanding concerning authority flows from this foundational and unalterable truth, which is the topic of my upcoming first chapter.

All of this points us toward the basic thesis of my book: when spiritual authority is unclear, the potential for division, strife, confusion, and darkness among God's people and the world is highly intensified, always lurking and waiting to erupt. While the church is my major focus, it's my conviction that the lack of understanding concerning spiritual authority is at the heart of most of the divisions within families, interpersonal relationships, churches, mission agencies, the workplace, government entities, and every form of community inside and outside the church.

It's my further conviction that the greatest hindrance to the gospel is not humanism, secularism, communism, or any other "ism." Rather, it's the lack of unity among God's people, the unity that Christ prayed for in John 17:20-23 (NASB) when He said, "I do not ask on behalf of these alone, but for those also who believe in Me through their word; that they may all be one; even as You, Father, are in Me and I in You, that they also may be in Us, so that the world may believe that You sent Me."

There can be no godly unity where there is no godly, loving, and responsible authority. This is why the Scriptures teach clearly and unequivocally about the authority in governments, in families, among servants and masters (employees and employers), and within churches. This is also why God is serious about punishing disrespect for and rebellion against authority.

Looking ahead, I will explore the subject of spiritual authority from several perspectives:

- Chapter 1 will deal with God as the source of all authority.

- Chapter 2 will define the animosity to authority by Satan and humanity.

- Chapter 3 will outline the concept of submission to authority as modeled in the Godhead.

- Chapter 4 will explain godly authority as it is applied to the world.

- Chapter 5 will consider godly authority as it is applied in the home.

- Chapter 6 will look at how male headship and authority were reinforced after the Fall.

- Chapter 7 will show how male headship and authority is supported in the New Testament.

- Chapters 8, 9, and 10 will explain how godly authority applies to marriage, parenting, and the role of women in the parental process.

- Chapter 11 will describe how godly authority applies to the godliness of children.

- Chapter 12 will look at the biblical description and explanation of godly authority in the Church.

- Chapters 13, 14, and 15 summarize the qualifications necessary to become an elder and tackles whether women can become elders in a church.

- Chapters 16 outlines the roles and responsibilities for women in the Church.

- Finally, chapters 17 and 18 outline how elders should be selected and their practical function in the Church.

So there's my roadmap. Thanks for joining me on this journey!

GOD AS THE SOURCE OF ALL AUTHORITY

God as the source of all authority stands on two indestructible pillars of truth:

1. The general and relentless teaching of all the Scripture on the absolute sovereignty of God.

2. The specific passages of Scripture that speak to all human authority deriving its justification and validation from God Himself.

---

1. The Absolute Sovereignty of God

Many theological works have thoroughly and decisively set forth the foundational scriptural truth that the God of the Bible is absolutely sovereign over all the affairs of men, women, and all created beings in the heavens and on earth and under the earth (Philippians 2:10).

Some of the major categories impacted by this subject are:

- God's sovereignty in creation

- God's sovereignty over human kingdoms

- God's sovereignty in man's salvation

- God's sovereignty over the Church

- God's sovereignty over the judgment of mankind

- God's sovereignty over His angelic hosts

- God's sovereignty over all principalities and powers
  of darkness in heavenly places

- God's sovereignty over eternity

For now, I want to zero in on God's sovereignty and His authority over all human governments and human society as described in Isaiah 40:1-11. The reason I've selected this passage is because it deals most specifically with this topic and represents the biblical principle of God's sovereignty clearly and powerfully:

> "Comfort, O comfort My people," says your God.
> "Speak kindly to Jerusalem;
> And call out to her, that her warfare has ended,
> That her iniquity has been removed,
> That she has received of the Lord's hand
> Double for all her sins."
>
> A voice is calling,
> "Clear the way for the Lord in the wilderness;
> Make smooth in the desert a highway for our God.
> "Let every valley be lifted up,
> And every mountain and hill be made low;
> And let the rough ground become a plain,
> And the rugged terrain a broad valley;
> Then the glory of the Lord will be revealed,
> And all flesh will see it together;
> For the mouth of the Lord has spoken."
> A voice says, "Call out."
> Then he answered, "What shall I call out?"
> All flesh is grass, and all its loveliness is like the
> flower of the field.
> The grass withers, the flower fades,

When the breath of the Lord blows upon it;
Surely the people are grass.
The grass withers, the flower fades,
But the word of our God stands forever.

Get yourself up on a high mountain,
O Zion, bearer of good news,
Lift up your voice mightily,
O Jerusalem, bearer of good news;
Lift it up, do not fear.
Say to the cities of Judah,
"Here is your God!"
Behold, the Lord God will come with might,
With His arm ruling for Him.
Behold, His reward is with Him
And His recompense before Him.
Like a shepherd He will tend His flock,
In His arm He will gather the lambs
And carry them in His bosom;
He will gently lead the nursing ewes.

In these first eleven verses of Isaiah 40, God expresses in comforting and loving terms His future plans for His people as manifested in the nation of Israel. There is much to understand concerning: God's forgiveness in verses 1-2; God's glorious and majestic revelation of Himself in verses 3-5; the message concerning man's temporary stay upon this earth contrasted with the unalterable word of God that "stands forever" in verses 6-8; and finally, God's intensely joyful good news of His coming to be with His people in power and glory while gently caring for them like a shepherd caring for His sheep in verses 9-11.

Nestled in this moving and glorious unfolding of His loving purposes for His people are several strong allusions to God's total sovereignty in the affairs of mankind. The first has to do with

God's judgment on the nation of Israel and His forgiveness of their "iniquity." Only a sovereign God has the authority to determine who rebels are and how they should be punished and for how long. Only a sovereign God has the authority to determine who should be forgiven and when that will happen.

* * *

Turning to specifics, God commands in Isaiah 40:2: "Speak kindly to Jerusalem; and call out to her, that her warfare has ended, that her iniquity has been removed, that she has received of the Lord's hand double for all her sins."

God's concern here is that evil be defeated in the lives and fellowship of His people. No human or any other created being has the authority to resist, limit, and overpower evil. Even the religious leaders who were sworn enemies of Jesus were correct in their theology when they accused Jesus of blasphemy because "who can forgive sins but God alone?" (Mark 2:7).

They were right but missed the obvious truth: Jesus is God, the Lord of the Universe. They missed this truth because of their sinful blindness, not realizing that the authority of the triune God over sin was made clear when John the Baptist introduced Jesus by saying, "Behold, the Lamb of God who takes away the sin of the world!" (John 1:29).

The second allusion or inference to God's absolute sovereignty is seen in the appropriate preparation necessary for a sovereign king to come to his people or lead his army. The way this king travels is to be made "smooth in the desert a highway for our God." This will include tremendous effort to "Let every valley be lifted up, and every mountain and hill be made low; and let the rough ground become a plain, and the rugged terrain a broad valley" (Isaiah 40:3-4).

That an earthly king should have his sovereignty acknowledged in this way is revealed in various historical documents, but in Isaiah, the king is referred to as "our God." As such, He is King of Kings and Lord of Lords above all others. When He returns, His glory will be revealed and "all flesh will see it together" (Isaiah 40:5). The truth of His absolute sovereignty is powerfully stated in the same verse, for "the mouth of the LORD has spoken." This is the same divine word that brought the world into being, as recorded in Genesis, chapter 1.

The third allusion to God's absolute sovereignty is expressed in His absolute control over the life breath of "all flesh" in verse 5 and how the "grass withers, the flower fades, when the breath of the LORD blows upon it" in verses 6-8. This truth finds its equally powerful expression in the apostle Paul's declaration to the philosophers in Athens in Acts 17:24-25:

> The God who made the world and all things in
> it, since He is LORD of heaven and earth, does
> not dwell in temples made with hands; nor is He
> served by human hands, as though He needed
> anything, since He Himself gives to all people life
> and breath and all things.

There can be no question that these statements declare God to be in control of all the affairs of mankind.

The fourth allusion in these first eleven verses to God's absolute sovereignty has to do with His ability to bring good news to a broken people. The intensity of this good news is heard in the following words from Isaiah 40:9, which I'll repeat here:

> Get yourself up on a high mountain O Zion,
> bearer of good news,
> Lift up your voice mightily, O Jerusalem, bearer
> of good news;

Lift it up, do not fear.
Say to the cities of Judah,
"Here is your God!"

That His rule and sovereignty make this good news possible is clear because the Lord God will come with power and might, but His sovereignty is joined with compassion and tenderness as a shepherd tending to His flock in verse 11:

Like a shepherd He will tend His flock,
In His arm He will gather the lambs
And carry them in His bosom;
He will gently lead the nursing ewes.

A shepherd has complete control of his flock of sheep. These domesticated animals are totally dependent on him and under his authority. This metaphor of the shepherd and his sheep is even more completely spoken by Jesus, when He says in John 10:11-15:

"I am the good shepherd; the good shepherd lays down His life for the sheep. He who is a hired hand, and not a shepherd, who is not the owner of the sheep, sees the wolf coming, and leaves the sheep and flees, and the wolf snatches them and scatters them. He flees because he is a hired hand and is not concerned about the sheep. I am the good shepherd, and I know My own and My own know Me, even as the Father knows Me and I know the Father; and I lay down My life for the sheep."

What greater news could we hear than the wonderful truth about our sovereign God, than that He is holy, good, compassionate, and tender? He protects us and cares for us. He has laid down His life for us.

* * *

Beginning with Isaiah 40:12, the prophet—under the inspiration of the Holy Spirit—moves from strong allusion to a powerful declaration of God's sovereignty in several crucial areas. The first refers to the process of creation. In verse 12, he asks rhetorically:

> Who has measured the waters in the hollow of
> His hand,
> And marked off the heavens by the span,
> And calculated the dust of the earth by the
> measure,
> And weighed the mountains in a balance and the
> hills in a pair of scales?

Not only does this passage unquestionably declare that God is the creator of this universe, but it also metaphorically reveals Him as so immense that this creation process was carried out at His workbench like a craftsman patiently toiling until his work was complete. For us, this points out the infinite greatness of a God who handcrafted this massive and incomprehensible universe into being.

Leading with another series of rhetorical questions, Isaiah points out that this sovereign God is the source of all wisdom, knowledge, and understanding as he asks in verses 13-14:

> Who has directed the Spirit of the LORD,
> Or as His counselor has informed Him?
> With whom did He consult and who gave Him
> understanding?
> And who taught Him in the path of justice and
> taught Him knowledge
> And informed Him of the way of understanding?

Isaiah now moves from these rhetorical questions to make several metaphorical statements about God's relationship to all the power and pomp of human government, geography, and organized authority in versus 15-17:

> Behold, the nations are like a drop from a bucket,
> And are regarded as a speck of dust on the scales;
> Behold, He lifts up the islands like fine dust.
>
> Even Lebanon is not enough to burn,
> Nor its beasts enough for a burnt offering.
>
> All the nations are as nothing before Him,
> They are regarded by Him as less than nothing
> and meaningless.

The contrast in these statements is stark and unquestionable. All that we think about humans being huge, powerful, and immensely significant is "nothing" to God.

Isaiah next reveals how absolutely ludicrous it is for us to make such a desperate effort to shrink God down to an idol that can be put on a shelf. Those who are wealthy and ludicrous make this idol out of gold and silver. Those who are poor and ludicrous make it out of a high-quality tree.

In almost mocking words Isaiah asks in verse 21:

> Do you not know? Have you not heard?
> Has it not been declared to you from the
> beginning?
> Have you not understood from the foundations
> of the earth?

Isaiah is calling us to consider how foolish we are to think that we have any control over God or have any capacity to "liken" Him or understand Him.

The prophet then brings it home with a powerful summary that proclaims God as the center, source, and goal of this entire universe and any and all of its inhabitants. In verse 22, he declares that the inhabitants of this earth are like grasshoppers to God, who uses the heavens as His personal tent with curtains. Isaiah further declares that all of mankind's accomplishments in his most exalted leaders are reduced by God to nothing.

The people see their rulers and judges as exhibiting power and permanence and security. Isaiah counters in verse 24 that not only are they not powerful, permanent, or a source of security, but:

> Scarcely have they been planted,
> Scarcely have they been sown,
> Scarcely has their stock taken root in the earth,
> But He merely blows on them, and they wither,
> And the storm carries them away like stubble.

Isaiah finishes this part of his discourse by turning to the majestic immensity of the heavens. These days, we know the universe contains billions of galaxies to the point that we can no longer comprehend its utter vastness. Isaiah asserts that God has created every star and leads them forth each night by number and names He has given them. The stars are all in place and none of them is missing "because of the greatness of His might and the strength of His power" (verse 26).

Isaiah, in verses 27-31 of this majestic 40th chapter, turns to the application of this indispensable and glorious truth about God's absolute sovereignty. He begins by raising the issue of humanity's complaint against God by His people—Israel—who have said, "My way is hidden from the LORD, and the justice due me escapes the notice of my God."

Isaiah reminds Israel of what they have been taught about their God with this gentle rebuke in verse 28:

Do you not know? Have you not heard?
The Everlasting God, the LORD, the Creator of the
ends of the earth
Does not become weary or tired.
His understanding is inscrutable.

This passage describing who God is can be likened to a refresher course in Theology Proper. Isaiah is declaring that there is no power shortage with God due to weariness. He reminds the people of Israel that God's understanding and wisdom are so far beyond what we could ever know that he has to use the term "inscrutable."

He also declares, contrary to their accusations, that God has always and continues to give "strength to the weary, and to him who lacks might He increases power" in verse 29. The heart of Isaiah's application is based on the acknowledgment that in this broken evil world, we all grow weary and tired and frequently stumble, including the most vigorous of us—the young. Secondly, he encourages and exhorts us that the key to being renewed in strength, perseverance, and even exultation is to wait or look for the Lord.

In one of the most beautiful and invigorating passages in the Bible, Isaiah pens verse 31, the final verse of Isaiah 40:

Yet those who wait for the LORD will gain new
strength;
They will mount up with wings like eagles,
They will run and not get tired,
They will walk and not become weary.

This is the core truth about submission to authority, which has everything to do with a sovereign God and our submission to Him. That is what it means to wait upon Him, to look for Him. We do not do anything or say anything that He is not leading us to do or say by His Spirit.

This foundational truth is what should undergird our motivation to submit to the authority of secondary agency, i.e. human authority. It's our confidence in God's absolute sovereignty that allows us to trust Him through the human authority that He has placed over us. This principle will drive the entire unfolding of my thesis. Without this fundamental truth, there is no basis for experiencing the "power of submission."

---

2. The Specific Teaching that God Is the Source of All Authority

To support this second indestructible pillar of truth regarding the concept that God, and God alone, is the only source of authority, I will be looking at two New Testament passages that will shape your mind and free your heart. As a reminder, it's my conviction that confusion in our thinking about authority is at the heart of most conflicts, strife, and division. It's also my conviction that a clear understanding of authority and a wholehearted commitment to live one's life under and in authority is one of the most freeing and joyful ways to live in this fallen world.

Romans 13:1-2 is the first passage I want you to consider, indicating that all authority has its source in God alone because the first two verses of this chapter establish several crucial principles concerning authority. Verses 3-7, which describe the application of the principles to government authority, will be talked about later. For now, I want to concentrate on Romans 13:1-2:

> Every person is to be in subjection to the governing authorities. For there is no authority except from God, and those which exist are established by God. Therefore whoever resists authority has opposed the ordinance of God; and they who

have opposed will receive condemnation upon themselves.

The first principle taught about authority in this passage is that "every person is to be in subjection to the governing authorities." That's black and white and clear as a bell.

In the Old Testament, we know that God was working in and through the nation of Israel. His authority was expressed through prophets who declared God's will to the people. Abraham, in Genesis 20:7, and Moses in Deuteronomy 18:15-18 were among the first to be appointed by God.

The Old Testament prophets were directly under God's authority. All others were under God's authority indirectly through the prophets. While judges and kings came into the history of God's people and provided governing authority, they were still under the authority of God through the prophets and were judged by God according to their obedience to His will and commands through them.

Unlike the Old Testament—where God's authority is expressed through individual prophets—in the New Testament God's authority is expressed through a *plurality* of human authority. When the Church was first formed in Acts 2, it was under the authority of the plurality of the apostles. This system of governance is continued with a plurality of eldership in all churches. The reason for this is because no human should *not* be under God's authority through His appointed human agents.

The second principle clearly stated in this passage is that "there is no authority except from God." This bedrock truth declares clearly that all of our thinking about authority must line itself up with this statement. Those in authority and those under authority should understand with great fear and reverence what God is teaching here.

When Pilate was adjudicating Jesus, he told Him that it would be to His advantage to speak to him since the Roman prefect had authority to execute Him or release Him.

Jesus' answer is pivotal to this discussion. He said to Pilate, "You would have no authority over Me, unless it had been given you from above" (John 19:11). In other words, Jesus, the Son of God who could call "twelve legions of angels" (Matthew 26:53) rushing to His aid, submitted Himself to Pilate's authority, which turned out to be unjust.

This did not change Jesus' obedience to that authority. Through this submission to Pilate's command, Jesus accomplished our redemption and purchased our salvation. Referring to the apostle Paul's argument in Romans, 20th century biblical scholar F. F. Bruce asserts that "Paul places the whole question on a very high plane. God Himself is the fount of all authority, and those who exercise authority on earth do so by delegation from Him."

Charles Hodge, a Presbyterian theologian from the 19th century, similarly states, "This is a very comprehensive proposition. All authority is of God . . . All human power is delegated and ministerial. This is true of parents, of magistrates, and of church officers." This foundational truth has clear and significant implications, the first being that any legitimate human authority that exists is "established by God." The second is that whoever resists this delegated human authority is resisting God and has, therefore, "opposed the ordinance of God." The third is that "they who oppose will receive condemnation upon themselves."

Hodge then more fully explains:

> Every person, who is in point of fact clothed with authority, is to be regarded as having a claim to obedience, founded on the will of God. In like manner, the authority of parents over their children, of husbands over their wives, of masters over their servants, is of God's ordination.

There is no limitation to the injunction in this verse, so far as the objects of obedience are concerned, although there is as to the extent of the obedience itself. That is, we are to obey all that is in actual authority over us, whether their authority be legitimate or usurped, whether they are just or unjust.

There is an extremely high spiritual principle being taught here: God, having all authority, takes His delegated authority on Earth very seriously. He does this to maintain order in the universe as well as in human society. He also does this for His own glory and purpose in restraining evil and establishing righteousness. His commitment to this principle is also seen in His punishment of those who oppose Him.

* * *

An interesting and telling event took place among the children of Israel as Moses was leading them through the wilderness. Aaron and Miriam, Moses' brother and sister, became disgruntled and disrespectful of Moses' leadership.

They essentially said, *Who do you think you are? Are you the only one through whom the Lord speaks? How about us? Doesn't He speak through us as well?*

What's interesting about this rebellion is that it took place through two godly people who were important and close to Moses. It's also significant that Moses did not defend himself. The scriptural testimony concerning him comes from Numbers 12:3: "Now the man Moses was very humble, more than any man who was on the face of the earth."

You might wonder if this humility characterizes any of us in a place of leadership. Nevertheless, this interaction turned into a terrifying experience for Aaron and Miriam when God called the three of them to the "tent of meeting" and appeared to them "in a pillar of cloud." As God stood in the pillar of cloud at the doorway to the tent, He pointedly called for Aaron and Miriam to come forward. When they came forward, God said to them in Numbers 12:6-8:

> Hear now my words:
> If there is a prophet among you,
> I, the LORD, shall make Myself known to him
> in a vision.
> I shall speak with him in a dream.
>
> Not so, with My servant Moses.
> He is faithful in all My household;
>
> With him I speak mouth to mouth,
> Even openly, and not in dark sayings,
> And he beholds the form of the LORD.
> Why then were you not afraid
> To speak against My servant, against Moses?

When God was through speaking, we're told that the "anger of the LORD burned against them and He departed" in verse 9. As He left, Miriam became leprous which may have been an indication that she was the instigator of this rebellion, similar to Eve with Adam.

Aaron, whose weakness was a desire to please the men responsible for the incident of the golden calf, saw what his passivity and weakness had brought on Miriam. To his credit, he repented and acknowledged their sin and pleaded for God's mercy regarding Miriam.

Moses, the target of this rebellion, also graciously pleaded for Miriam's healing, saying, "O God, heal her, I pray!" God listened to Moses' entreaty, but then He devised a punishment that would cause all of them to never forget the seriousness of Miriam's offense. He decreed that her disobedience required a public shaming and an acknowledgement of her sin. She was told to live alone outside the camp (a prescribed treatment of a leper, per Numbers 5:1-4) for a period of seven days, a standard time to deal with any uncleanness (Numbers 19:11).

This was such an important act of disobedience to God's way of submission to authority that He stopped the progress of approximately 2.5 million people in their trek toward the Promised Land. Everyone needed to understand this principle.

This story, which takes up the entire 12th chapter of Numbers, is a powerful example of how seriously God is committed to having His authority be respected on this earth. Given the tragic and terrifying breakdown of human society in our present-day world, mostly due to disrespect for God's authority, this is a crucial issue in all aspects of human experience.

Another powerful declaration of this principle is outlined in 1 Peter 2:13-3:7, an extended passage that's critical to our understanding of God's authority through His delegated agents. Because I will be referring to certain parts of Scripture, I've added the verse numbers:

> 13 Submit yourselves for the Lord's sake to every human institution, whether to a king as the one in authority, 14 or to governors as sent by him for the punishment of evildoers and the praise of those who do right. 15 For such is the will of God that by doing right you may silence the ignorance of foolish men.

> 16 Act as free men, and do not use your freedom as a covering for evil, but use it as bondslaves of God. 17 Honor all people, love the brotherhood, fear God, honor the king.

[18] Servants, be submissive to your masters with all respect, not only to those who are good and gentle, but also to those who are unreasonable. [19] For this finds favor, if for the sake of conscience toward God a person bears up under sorrows when suffering unjustly. [20] For what credit is there if, when you sin and are harshly treated, you endure it with patience? But if when you do what is right and suffer for it you patiently endure it, this finds favor with God.

[21] For you have been called for this purpose, since Christ also suffered for you, leaving you an example for you to follow in His steps, [22] who committed no sin, nor was any deceit found in His mouth; [23] and while being reviled, He did not revile in return; while suffering, He uttered no threats, but kept entrusting Himself to Him who judges righteously; [24] and He Himself bore our sins in His body on the cross, so that we might die to sin and live to righteousness; for by His wounds you were healed. [25] For you were continually straying like sheep, but now you have returned to the Shepherd and Guardian of your souls.

In the same way, you wives, be submissive to your own husbands so that even if any of them are disobedient to the word, they may be won without a word by the behavior of their wives, [2] as they observe your chaste and respectful behavior. [3] Your adornment must not be merely external—braiding the hair, and wearing gold jewelry, or putting on dresses; [4] but let it be the hidden person of the heart, with the imperishable quality of a gentle and quiet spirit, which is precious in the sight of God. ⁵For in this way in former times the holy women also, who hoped in God, used to adorn themselves, being submissive to their own husbands; ⁶just as Sarah obeyed Abraham, calling him lord, and you have become her children if you do what is right without being frightened by any fear.

⁷You husbands in the same way, live with your wives in an understanding way, as with someone weaker, since she is a woman; and show her honor as a fellow heir of the grace of life, so that your prayers will not be hindered.

This long passage from Peter's first letter is perhaps the most comprehensive section on the subject of authority in all of Scripture.

Note that in 1 Peter 2:11 the apostle refers to God's people as "aliens and strangers." This indicates our position in this world that is broken and in rebellion against its Creator. We are not to be part of that rebellion because our citizenship is in another country, as Hebrews 11:13-16 teaches us.

As such, we are not to live in "fleshly lusts which wage war against the soul" as God's Word further states in verse 11. "Fleshly lusts" refers to those desires that have their source in our humanity apart from God. They are desires born out of every effort to live our lives on our own without God.

It can be reasonably argued here that one of the ways we can abstain from fleshly lusts is to understand and live out God's principle of submission to His delegated human authorities. At the very least, this spirit of submission to authority would place a restraint on our innate, strong commitment to follow our own desires, do our own will, and go our own way.

In addition, this should remind us of our penchant for willfulness and encourage us to seek God's help to "check the rising doubt, the rebel sigh," as Irish poet George Croly wrote 150 years ago.

Peter, in verse 12, challenges us to "keep our behavior excellent among the Gentiles." We have a responsibility to display good deeds and thus silence their unfounded accusations against us. But even more importantly, as others observe those good deeds, they may "glorify God in the day of visitation."

This context leads us into Peter's discussion about human institutions and authority. Our submission to these God-ordained human authorities is one of the most powerful manifestations of God at work in us through our good deeds. Doing so also presents an obvious contrast to the prevalent rebellious attitudes of pagan humans and produces righteousness and peace in this dark and broken world.

* * *

The first part of verse 13 establishes the principle that underlies the entire position of this thesis: "Submit yourselves for the LORD's sake to every human institution."

The Greek word for the English word *submit* is *hupotasso*. Its various meanings include "to arrange under," which implies order—in this case, God's divine order. Another definition, according to *Thayer's Greek-English Lexicon*, means "to subject one's self, to obey: to submit to one's control; to yield to one's admonition or advice." The tense, voice, and mood of this verb is aorist in the Classical Greek, meaning that as a verb tense, the word expresses action, or, in the indicative mood, past action without reference to its completeness, duration, or repetition. In simpler terms, this means the verb tense is passive and imperative.

In his book, *Greek New Testament,* Henry Alford translates

this Greek word as "to be subjected." He then gives an expanded translation of the word, saying it's "to be in a condition of having been subjected." This nuance of the Greek text and grammar adds the power of God's transcendent order of things having to do with authority and submission. We submit ourselves because the Sovereign Lord of the universe has placed us in this position of submission. It's His plan and way for us. The word *submit* is not ambiguous or obscure but clearly establishes authority and submission to that authority as a foundational principle woven into the warp and woof of our creaturely existence.

The phrase *human institution* in 1 Peter 2:13 is a combination of two words: *anthropinos*, meaning "applied to things belonging to men or instituted by men," according to *Thayer;* and *ktsis,* meaning the act of founding, building, establishing; creation, thing created; the sum or aggregate of created things; an institution, ordinance.

This word implies an orderly process of creating, building, or establishing something, thus an institution or ordinance as opposed to something that is random or chaotic. The interpretation here is fairly simple: there are orderly and intentional creations of men for the purpose of governance and authority. These legitimate expressions of human authority are ordained by God and thus to be obeyed by us humans.

While the implication of order and harmony is implicit, the overarching motivation is "for the LORD's sake." That is, God is against all that is evil. Disorder and chaos are an evil in society and in His eyes. Therefore, to cooperate with Him and support His purposes through submission to His delegated human authority is to do it for Him and thus fulfill His will and purpose for human society.

Peter next moves to identify several areas of human society in which this principle of submission to delegated human authority is to be applied. In verses 13-17, he deals with civil authorities, and two important truths must be pointed out. The first is that this obedience to civil authorities is the will of God, and second, doing this obedience rightly will "silence the ignorance of foolish men," as Peter writes in verse 15.

The ignorance of foolish men consists of their belief that they can live their lives in defiance of God's authority and restraints and that they have the freedom to do as they please. The example of God's people acting with godly submission will help restrain the rebellious spirit that's prevalent in today's world and produces so much destruction and chaos.

God's Word shows us the foolishness and ignorance of this way of life and thus silences it—not completely but substantially. In addition, God acknowledges that we as His people have been set free from the evil control of this world and the forces of darkness, but we are not to use that glorious freedom as any excuse or covering of evil deeds in our lives.

Instead, we are to think of ourselves as bondslaves of God, totally and joyfully under His authority, which frees us to "honor all people, love the brotherhood, fear God, honor the king" (verse 17). Underlying every act of submission to legitimate human authority is submission to God Himself in and through that authority. Our trust and hope are not in any human agency. It is only in God, who is in control of every human agency and uses it for His own purposes and glory.

In verses 18-20, Peter deals with a specific human institution—slavery. While I won't be dealing with the entire scope of biblical truth about slavery, it's noteworthy that through Peter (and Jesus and Paul as well), the Holy Spirit is way more concerned about the righteous response of God's people in slavery than how to free them from it.

Note that the Greek word for "servants" that Peter uses— *oiketas*—is a more restricted term than *doulos*, which refers to "a house servant, or one holding closer relations to the family than other slaves," according to *Thayer.*

Edwin Blum, author of *The Expositor's Bible Commentary,* wrote, "People became slaves in various ways—through war, bankruptcy, sale by themselves, sale by parents, or by birth. Slaves normally could look forward to freedom after a certain period of service and often after the payment of a price." It's also important to note that in 1st century Rome, much of what we would call "work" or physical labor was done by slaves. In our more affluent society, this message would be to "employees" rather than slaves. The application of this passage is the same for both.

Peter now returns to the word *hupotasso,* which means to subject or put in subjection. This time, however, the apostle uses the present, middle participle, which could be translated "continue subjecting yourselves."

This participle keys off the action of the previous paragraph, but perhaps even more specifically of the verb form in verse 13. In other words, this subjecting of one's self is a continuation of the principle established in the broad, once-for-all action of verse 13, which indicates a condition of subjection to all appropriate authority established by God through human agency.

This idea is reinforced by the phrase "in all fear." Most translations tie this phrase to fearing or having respect for your masters/employers. While there is some truth in this, it's clear to me that this is intended to be a healthy fear of God. He is the one who established this principle and is the source of all authority. What Peter has written is quite similar to Paul's command that wives are to be submissive to their own husbands "as to the LORD." Our fear of God should be the most powerful incentive to obey His command to submit to and respect those in authority over us.

This important distinction is supported by several facts revealed in the ensuing paragraph. First, the word used here for master—*despotais*—is where we get our English word *despot.* *Thayer* asserts that this word "was strictly the correlative of slaves, *doulos,* and hence denoted absolute ownership and uncontrolled power." Being under this much control is, humanly speaking, a terrifying position to be in. Only a fear of and trust in a sovereign, loving Father can sustain one in such a position. Second, this submission includes not only those masters/employers who are good, understanding, and gentle, but those who are unreasonable as well.

This last English word is somewhat weak. The Greek word is *skolios,* which literally means "crooked" or "curved." Metaphorically the word has come to mean perverse, wicked, or unfair. Peter is fully aware of the suffering this kind of submission engenders. In both verses 19 and 20, he declares that suffering unjustly for doing what is right ushers us into the realm of God that is characterized by His grace, lovingkindness, goodwill, and favor.

In other words, God is pleased and graciously supports us in this suffering because when we bear up under sorrows and endure maltreatment with patience, we become powerful agents of His grace that is expressed to this unfair overseer. Our fear of God and our joyful submission to His sovereignty strengthens and frees us to submit to whatever delegated human authority under which He has placed us.

Quite a few years ago our son, David, came to me greatly disturbed about the rather bizarre behavior of his boss, the company owner. The boss had often expressed great appreciation for David and his work, but any time my son would raise a question about a policy or decision relating to the business, his boss would throw a fit, complete with yelling and anger. These outbursts lasted not just for a few minutes but sometimes would go on for several hours.

After listening to my son for a while and asking several questions, I told him, "This sure sounds like an intolerable situation." Then I grabbed a Bible and read to him this passage after telling him that I knew this would be difficult to hear, given what he had described, but God used this passage to give him the strength he needed to endure this bizarre and unfair behavior from his boss.

Here's where David's story takes an unexpected turn. A few months later, my son told me that he started arriving at work at 6 a.m., before anyone else, and would pray for this man before starting his workday. One morning, the owner/boss arrived early as well, and he asked my son why he had come to work so early.

"I've come early to pray for you," my son replied.

His boss was stunned. "Why?" he asked.

"Because I'm asking God to help you with your anger issues and to fill you with God's peace," my son said boldly.

His boss nodded and seemed to appreciate his concern. Sometime later, our son left that employment for another position that became available. I wish I could tell you that that man became a follower of Jesus, but I don't know that. What I do know is this: this man experienced God's grace and respect through our son when he deserved neither. I am confident that man will never be able to escape that encounter with God.

* * *

Peter's treatise on authority takes a dramatic turn that connects us to Jesus and His own submission to authority. The reason we should be willing to suffer unjustly is because we "have been called for this purpose." And this purpose is to follow Jesus and His example, who "also suffered for [us]" (versus 21).

The amazing thing about Jesus suffering unjustly is that He "committed no sin, nor was any deceit found in His mouth" (verse 22). It's one thing for us who are broken and sinful to suffer unjustly, but it's quite another thing for the spotless, perfect Son of God to do so. Even in His absolute perfection in His suffering unjustly, "while being reviled, He did not revile in return, while suffering He uttered no threats" (verse 23).

Jesus made no effort to justify or protect Himself. He also made no effort to point out the unjust treatment of Pilate and the Jews as an excuse to resist their authority and call down twelve legions of angels to deliver Him, which He had the power to do. The alternative action that Jesus chose was to "keep entrusting Himself to Him who judges righteously" (verse 23). The answer to all of our questions about why we are required to submit to authority begins with this entrusting ourselves to a Sovereign God who controls all in authority and who "judges righteously" (also verse 23).

Now comes the pinnacle of the truth being taught here about submission to authority. Because Jesus was willing to submit Himself to the authority of God His Father, and through Him to Pilate, the Roman Governor, we read this in verse 24, "He Himself bore our sins in His body on the cross, so that we might die to sin and live to righteousness; for by His wounds you were healed."

In other words, Jesus' suffering on the cross brought about our redemption from "continually straying like sheep" to returning "to the Shepherd and Guardian" of our souls as described at the end of 1 Peter 2.

The implication and application of this passage is clear: submission to God's delegated authority in this world can result in unjust suffering. When that happens, God will use it redemptively through us just as He did for Jesus His Son. This doesn't mean that we, in some way, pay atonement for our sins like Jesus did, but it does mean that God can and will use our unjust suffering to draw people to the redemption found in Christ Jesus through His death on the cross.

This astounding truth is explained further in the first two verses of chapter 3. Peter begins by exhorting wives to be submissive to their own husbands. This is another expression of God's delegated authority and submission to that authority. Again, this submission may result in suffering because of an unbelieving husband who is "disobedient to the word."

The phrase "in the same way," which starts chapter 3, refers to the original verb in 1 Peter 2:13, which is to "be in a condition of having been subjected, be subjected." This is a God-ordained position in which God has placed you and me alike.

Your submission to your husband, if you are a woman married to an unbelieving spouse, means that God will redemptively use your attitude to win your husband "without a word." This will happen as he observes your pure and respectful behavior and will be effective because your husband will see that you fear God and because of Him, you respectfully submit to your husband's God-ordained authority. This is the most powerful way to cooperate with God in the salvation of your husband.

Some years ago, my wife, Grace, and I were sitting at a long table in a suburb of Tokyo, Japan. We had just finished breakfast with nineteen Japanese women who had recently given their hearts and lives to Jesus. Sitting with us were the two faithful, godly, and single female missionaries who had led these nineteen women to Christ.

The missionaries introduced me as their pastor and Grace as my wife and asked the women if they had any questions they wanted to ask me about their faith and their walk with God.

One of the women, who seemed to be speaking for all of them, told us that their husbands were only interested in their work and had no time to think about God. They wanted to know, now that they were Christians, what they should do to help their husbands come to know and trust Jesus. They also indicated that their husbands not only had no time for God, but they had no time for them as their wives either.

I told them to open their Bibles to 1 Peter 3:1-6. I indicated to them that this passage had to be hard to hear, but this section of Scripture was the best thing I could tell them.

I gave these women time to read these six verses in their Japanese Bibles. After they had finished reading, some of them began to quietly weep and the room turned quiet. I asked the American missionaries what was happening. They talked to the women in Japanese and asked them why they were weeping.

The Japanese women, they said, were crying because this truth from God's Word was difficult to hear and understand. But they also said that deep in their hearts, they knew the start of 1 Peter 3 was true and they needed to be thankful that they were hearing this message from God because now they knew what He wanted them to do.

Twenty-five years later, one of those missionaries called to tell me that she had just heard from one of those nineteen women. This dear Japanese wife had written to tell her missionary friend that her husband had just received Jesus as his Savior and Lord. The godly and respectful attitude and behavior of this woman was used of God to bring her work-obsessed husband to repentance and faith.

God's ways work. His word is true. We can trust Him. And when we obey Him about this issue of submission to authority, we put ourselves in the best possible position to see God work in power and love.

This passage from two key chapters in 1 Peter shines a spotlight on the power of submission. Sure, there are questions and issues of application that I haven't dealt with, but a key principle of God's eternal truth is clearly and amazingly revealed. When rightly understood and applied, submission to God's ordained authority sets in motion God's redemptive purposes and actions in the lives of human beings no matter where they are in their various experiences and expressions.

Anytime you submit to God's authority, however, you can expect to catch the attention of the Adversary, which is the focus of my next chapter.

THE HATRED OF AUTHORITY
BY SATAN AND HUMANS

S atan hates God's authority, and I will clearly state that he and the demons under his jurisdiction have rebelled against Him since the dawn of Creation.

As with many important doctrines of Scripture, the Book of Genesis provides the foundation for our understanding of Satan and his relationship to God's authority. In the third chapter, Satan takes the form of a serpent and embarks on a discourse of deceit that undermines and refutes God's authority and Word as expressed to Adam and Eve in the Garden of Eden.

The deceiver first asks, "Indeed, has God said, 'You shall not eat from any tree of the garden'?" (Genesis 3:1).

The word "indeed" may not look like any big deal to anybody, but Satan used this word as an expression of surprise as well as incredulity that God would prevent Adam and Eve from eating from "any" tree. This subtle but powerful strategy caused Eve to doubt God's goodness and His right to impose any restriction. This significant undermining and weakening of God's authority, which was deceptively hidden, probably sounded like an "innocent" question to Eve.

The effectiveness of this strategy is revealed in Eve's response. She first downplays God's generous indication that they could eat from "any" tree in the garden (2:16) with a bland, generic statement indicating no excitement or evidence of thanksgiving. In Genesis 3:2-3, Eve responds to the serpent in this manner:

"From the fruit of the trees of the garden we may eat; but from the fruit of the tree which is in the middle of the garden, God has said, 'You shall not eat from it or touch it, or you will die.'"

What Eve did was embellish God's restriction of not eating of the tree of the knowledge of good and evil by adding that she and Adam were not to "touch it" since in the previous chapter, God said "the tree of the knowledge of good and evil you shall not eat, for in the day that you eat from it you will surely die" (Genesis 2:17).

Why Eve said they were not to touch it, I'm not sure, but Satan's subtle approach found a soft spot in Eve's heart. What Satan did was shrewdly remind her that God had no right to limit her choice and freedom in any way.

Following this exchange, Satan abandons all subtlety and brazenly contradicts God's clear word when he immediately replies, "You surely will not die" in Genesis 3:4.

He next expands this lie by appealing to Eve's pride and telling her that if she will only disregard God's authority and make her own choices, then she will have her eyes opened and "be like God, knowing good and evil" (Genesis 3:5). This temptation of Eve by Satan to be like God by appealing to her pride is a repetition of the process that Satan experienced before the creation of man. This is inferred by a composite of scriptural references that reveal Satan as God's adversary—which is where the meaning of the name "Satan" comes from—and relentless enemy.

Wayne Grudem, in his book *Systematic Theology*, rightly indicates that God's assessment of all His creative works as "very good" included the angelic beings, of which Satan was one. Grudem then relates how in Genesis 3 Satan was the tempter to pride and rebellion against God. "Therefore," he inferred, "sometime between the events of Genesis 1:31 and Genesis 3:1, there must have been a rebellion in the angelic world with many angels turning against God and becoming evil."

One other passage from God's Word will prove helpful in understanding the rebellion of Satan and his demons against God's authority. In his letter to the church at Ephesus, Paul wrote this:

> Finally, be strong in the LORD and in the strength of His might. Put on the full armor of God, so that you will be able to stand firm against the schemes of the devil. For our struggle is not against flesh and blood, but against the rulers, against the powers, against the world forces of this darkness, against the spiritual forces of wickedness in the heavenly places.
>
> —Ephesians 6:10-12

This passage dramatically describes an entire spiritual world of evil governed by demonic rulers and authorities. That Satan and his demons have developed a complete authority structure that is opposed to God and His authority is abundantly evident and provides the context for a discussion about the hatred of God's authority by an unbelieving humanity.

There's a remarkable revelation of the unbelieving world's attitude toward God's authority in the second Psalm:

> Why are the nations in an uproar
> And the peoples devising a vain thing?
> The kings of the earth take their stand
> And the rulers take counsel together
> Against the LORD and against His Anointed,
> saying,
> "Let us tear their fetters apart
> And cast away their cords from us!"
>
> —Psalm 2:1-3

This psalm in sweeping language indicates an intense and irrational hatred of God's rule in this world by the unanimous and organized society of humanity. Derek Kidner, author of *Psalms 1-72*, observes, "The initial *Why* sets the tone of its approach, one of astonishment at the senseless rejection of God's rule and ruler."

Its intensity is felt in the phrase "in an uproar" in verse 1. This is the picture of godless humanity in a rage and turmoil like the churning of the ocean in a violent storm. This coalition of rebellion includes the nations; those who are united together politically, socially, and culturally; peoples of all races; and every individual on this planet.

The kings who represent human, worldly power take their stand and by doing so, they lead the people under their authority to unite in this raging rebellion. The rulers who represent all kinds of leadership sit and take counsel together against the Lord and His Anointed. This may be a raging inferno of godless hatred, but it's not random and chaotic. Rather, it's thoughtful, calculating, and devious.

These dramatic words indicate a united and unanimous spirit, purpose, and implementation of rebellion against God's authority. The action of all humanity is clear: they are going to "tear their fetters apart" and "cast away their cords from us" (verse 3). The fetters and cords refer to God's control and authority under which they writhe in anger and hatred.

Verse 1 is a reminder of how irrational this action is since their plotting is foolish and useless. The macrocosm of all humanity is manifested in the microcosm of God's people in Jeremiah 5:3, 5, which states:

> O LORD, do not Your eyes look for truth?
> You have smitten them, but they did not weaken;
> You have consumed them, but they refused to
> take correction.

They have made their faces harder than rock;
They have refused to repent . . .

I will go to the great and will speak to them,
For they know the way of the LORD
And the ordinance of their God.
But they too, with one accord have broken the
yoke
And burst the bonds.

Professing to follow God is not enough. Rebellion is the indication of false profession (Matthew 7:21-23).

Peter, in his second epistle, refers to the ungodly and unrighteous as "those who indulge the flesh in its corrupt desires and despise authority. Daring, self-willed, they do not tremble when they revile angelic majesties" (2:10). Paul alludes to this despising and hatred of authority when he writes to Timothy:

But realize this, that in the last days difficult
times will come. For men will be lovers of self,
lovers of money, boastful, arrogant, revilers, *disobedient to parents* . . .
—2 Timothy 3:1-2 with italics for emphasis

A prominent commentator on television recently produced an entire hour on the breakdown of authority in the home and its devastating impact on children and society at large. Many critics of our educational system wonder if public schooling can survive as a viable strategy to educate our children because the main destructive force in the classroom is the increasing disintegration of authority.

I believe there are two main reasons for this distrust and outright hatred of authority. The first is a characteristic of our flesh—living our lives apart from God. This began with distrust of God's authority by Eve and Adam when they agreed with Satan's lie that God was withholding good from them by denying them access to the tree of the knowledge of good and evil. Since that time in the Garden, distrust and hatred of God's authority has grown and permeated every segment of our human society and every corner of our hearts and minds.

C. S. Lewis gave us a valuable insight into this human hatred of authority in his autobiography, *Surprised by Joy*. Describing the trauma of his conversion to theism, the British theologian and apologist indicated that what he hated most in his unbelieving state was any interference with his plans or desires. His resistance stemmed from his view of God as "the Great Interferer." Lewis also referred to himself as the most reluctant convert in all of England, figuratively being carried kicking and screaming into the kingdom of God.

Most of us would be reluctant to admit this about ourselves, but as Isaiah wrote over twenty-five hundred years ago, "All of us like sheep have gone astray. Each of us has turned to his own way" (Isaiah 53:6).

The second reason for men and women's hatred of authority is the abject and sometimes devastating failure of those in authority. How many children are sent down a rebellious path by the abuse, abandonment, or neglect of their mother or father or both? How many women have embraced a life that they can control apart from God because a husband had abused or abandoned them? How many citizens have become cynical and distrustful of authority because government officials have lied, cheated, and abused their public trust when they should have been serving the people in their jurisdiction?

When those in authority violate the sacred trust of love, care, and protection, people are more than ready to believe their own innate aversion to authority and Satan's lies about God and His authority. As a result, we have a human society that is characterized by Paul's words in Romans 1:28-32:

And just as they did not see fit to acknowledge God any longer, God gave them over to a
depraved mind, to do those things which are not
proper, being filled with all unrighteousness,
wickedness, greed, evil; full of envy, murder,
strife, deceit, malice; they are gossips, slanderers,
haters of God, insolent, arrogant, boastful, inven-
tors of evil, disobedient to parents, without understanding, untrustworthy, unloving, unmerciful;
and although they know the ordinance of God,
that those who practice such things are worthy
of death, they not only do the same, but also give
hearty approval to those who practice them.

Given this innate hatred of authority by human beings, there
needs to be a powerful case made for the crucial need for a godly,
trustworthy, and loving authority in our lives, in our families, in
the Church, and in our world.

The foundation for making this case rests solidly on the nature
of God Himself, which is why authority and submission is modeled
in the Godhead, as I discuss in my next chapter.

AUTHORITY AND SUBMISSION MODELED IN THE GODHEAD

The relationship of authority in the Godhead—His divine nature—is clearly taught and exampled in the Scriptures.

The expression of authority and submission to authority is unequivocally declared in the relationship between God the Father and God the Son. The Son of God did not become the Son in Bethlehem when Jesus was born to Mary. He has been and is the *eternal* Son of God.

What happened is that the eternal Son of God became the Son of Man at Bethlehem. This concept of authority and submission in the Godhead rests on four supporting pillars in the Scriptures:

1. The first pillar is the implied authority inherent in the relationship of Father and Son.

2. The second pillar is the clear statements of Jesus in the New Testament that declare His submission to the Father.

3. The third pillar is the passages of Scripture that explicitly teach the Son's submission to the Father.

4. The fourth pillar is the clear indication that the Holy Spirit does His divine work in submission to both Father and Son.

Here's the upshot of this: authority is an inherent aspect of the relationships within the Trinity.

A key text on this subject is found in Paul's letter to the Ephesians (3:14-15):

> For this reason, I bow my knees before the
> Father, from whom every family in heaven and on
> earth derives its name.

The whole concept of a family with a father in leadership flows out of the relationships in the Godhead. The relationship between the Father and Son is displayed in so many passages of Scripture that we can only refer to a sampling of their astonishing number. One that stands out to me is God's promise to deliver Israel—His people—that's found in Isaiah 9:6. This verse, with italics added by me, is centered on His declaration that:

> For a child will be born to us, *a son will be given*
> *to us;*
> And the government will rest on His shoulders;
> And His name will be called Wonderful
> Counselor, Mighty God,
> Eternal Father, Prince of Peace.

Many commentators ignore the significance of "a son will be given to us," but the overwhelming importance of this is seen in perhaps the most famous and surely the most-quoted verse in the Bible: John 3:16, which states, "For God so loved the world that He gave His only begotten Son."

Although many people stop there, John 3:17 shares a compelling thought about the Son being *sent* to earth for our salvation:

> For God did not send the Son into the world to
> judge the world, but that the world might be
> saved through Him.

And consider this from Romans 8:32:

> He who did not spare His own Son, but delivered
> Him over for us all, how will He not also with
> Him freely give us all things?

These Scriptures declare that the Father has given, sent, and delivered the Son, which to me indicates the loving authority of the Father over the Son, which effects the salvation and deliverance of His people who put their trust in Him as Savior and Lord.

In Psalm 2:6-7, God the Father answers the futile rebellion of the nations and kings by saying:

> "But as for Me, I have installed my King
> Upon Zion, my holy mountain." . . .
> "He said to me, 'You are my Son,
> Today I have begotten you.'"

While it's true that this passage refers to the Davidic kingdom in David's time, it's also true that God's Word was fulfilled most completely in the Son of David, God's Messiah (the Anointed One).

As Derek Kidner, author of *Psalms 1-72*, comments, "For any earthly king, this form of address could bear only the lightest interpretation, but the New Testament holds us to its full value which excludes the very angels, to leave only one candidate in possession."

Kidner rightly points us to the first chapter of Hebrews to establish this psalm as referring to God's Son—the Messiah, Jesus. The author of Hebrews is seeking to establish the superiority of Jesus Christ over the Old Covenant and over all angelic beings. This he does, beginning in verse 1 with majestic and powerful rhetoric. This is such a pivotal passage of Scripture that I will include the first eight verses:

> God, after He spoke long ago to the fathers in the
> prophets in many portions and in many ways, in
> these last days has spoken to us in His Son, whom

He appointed heir of all things, through whom also He made the world. And He is the radiance of His glory and the exact representation of His nature, and upholds all things by the word of His power. When He had made purification of sins, He sat down at the right hand of the Majesty on high, having become as much better than the angels, as He has inherited a more excellent name than they.

For to which of the angels did He ever say,

> "You are My Son,
> Today I have begotten You"?

And again,

> "I will be a Father to Him
> And He shall be a Son to Me"?

And when He again brings the firstborn into the world, He says,

> "And let all the angels of God worship Him."

And of the angels He says,

> "Who makes His angels winds,
> And His ministers a flame of fire."

But of the Son He says,

> "Your throne, O God, is forever and ever,
> And the righteous scepter is the scepter of His kingdom."

The implied authority of God the Father over God the Son is abundantly clear in this passage, which brings me to make several summary statements:

- The Father initiates all communication.

- The Father appoints the Son as the heir of all things.

- The Father makes the world through the Son.

- The Father gives the Son the place of honor at His right hand.

- The Father takes the responsibility of being the Father to His Son.

- The Father establishes the honor of the Son by commanding His angels to worship Him, and giving Him the throne and the scepter of His kingdom.

When it is written that God has spoken to us in these last days "in His Son," the word *His* is not in the Greek text and there is no article. The literal translation would be "in Son."

Bishop Brooke Foss Westcott, a British biblical scholar from the 19th century, said, "The absence of the article fixes attention upon the nature and not the personality of the Mediator of the new revelation. God spake to us in one who has this character that He is Son."

Arthur Pink, a biblical scholar and pastor in the early 20th century, writes similarly, "*In Son* has reference to that which characterized God's revelation. The thought of the contrast is that God, who of old had spoken *prophetwise,* now speaks *sonwise.*"

The point of this discussion is that inherent in being a son is the concept of submission to the authority of a father. Wayne Grudem in *Systematic Theology* affirms this, writing, "So we may say that the role of the Father in creation and redemption has been to plan and direct and send the Son and Holy Spirit. This is not surprising, for it shows that the Father and the Son relate to one another as a father and son relate to one another in a human family: the father directs and has authority over the son, and the son obeys and is responsive to the directions of the father."

Another important aspect of this truth is that this relationship of God the Father and God the Son wasn't just true during Jesus' sojourn on the earth but is, in fact, eternally true. God has always existed as God the Father, God the Son, and God the Holy Spirit. These relationships in the Godhead and the roles they manifest are not interchangeable, nor can they be reversed. If they were then "the Father would have ceased to be the Father and the Son would have ceased to be the Son," as Grudem noted.

While this text establishes the authority of the Father over the Son, it also establishes the Son as equal with the Father in the way it refers to the Son as the "radiance of His [the Father's] glory and the exact representation of His nature."

The Greek word for radiance is *aupaugasma*. Interpretations vary between effulgence and reflection. Effulgence has the sense of something that radiates or "out-rays" from a source of light, rather than that which only reflects light. Henry Alford, author of the *Greek Testament*, which he wrote in 1859, comes down on the side of effulgence when he opines, "the Son of God is, in this his essential majesty, the expression, and the sole expression, of the divine Light—not, as in his Incarnation, but its reflexion."

Marvin Richardson Vincent, in his *Word Studies in the New Testament*, writes in a similar vein as he relates that the consensus of the Greek "Fathers" is on the side of effulgence, and that this consensus is "of great weight." He also quotes Bernhard Weiss: "God lets His glory issue from Himself, so that there arises thereby a *light-being* like Himself."

The next phrase continues the truth of the Son's equality with the Father, affirming that He is "the exact representation of His nature." The Greek word *caraktaer* means "the exact expression (the image) of any person or thing, precise reproduction in every respect." The word translated as "nature" in the NASB is *upos-*

tasis, which has a meaning in this context as "the substantial quality, nature, of any person or thing."

It would be difficult to imagine a clearer expression in the English language of the meaning of the Greek text because it unquestionably fits Jesus' answer to Philip's request: "LORD, show us the Father, and it is enough for us" (John 14:8).

In reply, Jesus said to him, "Have I been so long with you, and yet you have not come to know Me, Philip? He who has seen Me has seen the Father; how can you say, 'Show us the Father'?" (John 14:9).

This also fits with what Paul writes to the church at Philippi about Jesus "who although He existed in the form of God, did not regard equality with God a thing to be grasped" in Philippians 2:6.

This truth of the *equality* of the Son with the Father is crucial, specifically in its juxtaposition with His *submission* to the *authority* of the Father. I say it's crucial because of the way human society interprets authority as superiority and submission as inferiority.

There is man's way of thinking, and there is God's way of thinking. Isaiah, the prophet of God, spoke God's word:

> "For My thoughts are not your thoughts,
> Nor are your ways My ways," declares the LORD.
>
> "For as the heavens are higher than the earth,
> So are My ways higher than your ways
> And My thoughts than your thoughts."
> —Isaiah 55:8-9

There is significant confusion about the issue of God's authority in the Church at large. This is due, to a great extent, to the reality that we listen to man's ways and thoughts in our culture more than we listen to God's ways and thoughts. An excellent summary of this deep and intricate relationship within the Trinity is given by Wayne Grudem when he writes:

This truth about the Trinity has sometimes been summarized in the phrase "ontological equality but economic subordination," where the word *ontological* means "being." Another way of expressing this more simply would be to say "equal in being but subordinate in role."

Both parts of this phrase are necessary to a true doctrine of the Trinity: If we do not have ontological equality, not all the persons are fully God. But if we do not have economic subordination, then there is no inherent difference in the way the three persons relate to one another, and consequently we do not have the three distinct persons existing as Father, Son, and Holy Spirit for all eternity.

I would also add that if we do not have economic subordination, we have no clear model for the concept of authority. Because authority and submission to authority exist in the Godhead, we can understand this as the foundation for all other relationships of authority and submission, e.g. husband and wife, parents and children, masters and slaves, civic leaders and citizens, employers and employees, and elders and congregation.

The Clear Words of Jesus Concerning His Submission to the Father

Let me begin with what appears to be a discussion between the Father and the Son prior to the Incarnation. This discussion is recorded in the book of Hebrews 10:5-7,

Therefore, when He comes into the world, He says,

"Sacrifices and offering you have not desired,
But a body you have prepared for Me;

In whole burnt offerings and sacrifices for sin
you have taken no pleasure.

Then I said, 'Behold, I have come (In the scroll
of the book it is written of Me)

To do your will, O God.'"

This is one of those rare, mysterious, and astonishing passages of Scripture where the Spirit of God pulls back the curtain of divine knowledge and relationship and allows us to reverently look into the heart and plan of the triune God. We are able to behold the awesome unity and relationship of the Father and the Son. We see the Son's understanding of the Father's heart and plan for His redemption of fallen humanity.

The Father never intended the sacrifices of the Old Covenant to satisfy His judgement of our sin and the sin-infected universe. Father and Son together have devised an infinite sacrifice for sin that is abundantly sufficient to satisfy the just demands of an infinitely holy God. This involves the sacrifice of the incarnate Son of God, the Lamb of God as John the Baptist referred to Him in John 1:29, to take away the sin of the world.

For this to take place, the Father is going to "prepare" a body for His Son. This refers to Jesus' miraculous birth through the virgin Mary into this world. This is the glorious event we celebrate at Christmas. The Son makes it clear that His coming into the world is to do the Father's will. As the eternal Son of God, He has always been ready to submit to the Father to carry out His plan.

These words of the pre-incarnate Christ describe His eternal relationship and role with the Father. Arthur Pink puts it this way:

It was necessary that Christ's consent should be then given, even from everlasting, and that as God made a promise to Him for us, so also that He should give consent unto God . . . not only to the end that He might be privy to the first design and contrivement of our salvation, and know the bottom of God's mind and heart in it . . . but also in this respect, that His very own consent should go to it from the first, even as soon as His Father should design it.

Pink's insight is crucial in understanding how authority and submission work in God's kingdom. The submission of the one under authority is volitional, that is, it involves the free giving of one's self to the authority of the one exercising that authority. The one in authority is not controlling or coercive of the one *under* his authority.

As mysterious as it seems, this free exchange and relationship of submission and authority is in complete harmony with the absolute sovereignty of the triune God. This is beyond our minds to comprehend, but it should bring us to our knees in the doxological utterance of Paul:

Oh, the depth of the riches both of the wisdom and knowledge of God! How unsearchable are His judgments and unfathomable His ways!
—Romans 11:33

This moving and powerful revelation of the Son's expressed eternal submission to the Father is manifested in His life here on earth. There are multiple passages in the New Testament where Jesus expresses in the clearest and strongest terms His submission to His Father's will. The following passages are a sampling:

- **John 4:34**: "Jesus said to them, 'My food is to do the will of Him who sent Me and to accomplish His work.'"

- **John 5:19**: "Therefore Jesus answered and was saying to them, 'Truly, truly, I say to you, the Son can do nothing of Himself, unless it is something He sees the Father doing; for whatever the Father does, these things the Son also does in like manner.'"

- **John 5:30**: "I can do nothing on My own initiative. As I hear, I judge; and My judgement is just, because I do not seek My own will but the will of Him who sent me."

In addition to many other passages, the poignant and powerful and awesome words of Jesus in Gethsemane are indicative of the depth of Jesus' submission to His Father:

> Then Jesus came with them to a place called Gethsemane, and said to His disciples, "Sit here while I go over there and pray." And He took with Him Peter and the two sons of Zebedee and began to be grieved and distressed. Then He said to them, "My soul is deeply grieved, to the point of death; remain here and keep watch with Me."
> And He went a little beyond them, and fell on His face and prayed, saying, "My Father, if it is possible, let this cup pass from Me; yet not as I will, but as You will."
> —Matthew 26:36-39

This prayer of Jesus to His Father, which is also recorded in Mark 14 and Luke 22, indicates the almost overwhelming temptation to give in to His own feelings regarding the anxiety and stress He felt as He looked for a way out of this terrible and awesome hour when He would take upon Himself all of the evil of humanity and the fallen universe. The worst part of taking on Himself all of this evil was the contemplation of the necessary separation from the Father at the moment of His sacrifice for our sins.

His anguished cry, "My God, My God, why have You forsaken me?" (Mark 15:34) reveals to our shuddering acknowledgment the horror He was anticipating in His prayer in the Garden. It was in this moment that Jesus' submission to His Father was put to its extreme test. His unshakable submission made it possible for Him to complete His glorious and powerful work of salvation for the forgiveness of our sins.

Passages of Scripture That Explicitly or Implicitly Teach the Son's Submission to the Father

Ephesians 4:1-6, part of the most comprehensive passage in Scripture on the Church, begins with a call to a worthy walk in Christ for God's people. This worthy walk is based on an amazing unity that flows from God Himself.

After imploring us as God's people to fulfill our part in "[preserving] the unity of the Spirit in the bond of peace," Paul gives us the foundation of that unity in the triune God and their respective roles and responsibilities. His declarations about each member of the Trinity manifests an indestructible unity in the Godhead:

> There is one body and one Spirit . . . one Lord, one
> faith, one baptism, one God and Father of all who
> is over all and through all and in all.
> —Ephesians 4:4-6

The one body and one Spirit referred to is more completely described in 1 Corinthians 12:12-13:

> For even as the body is one and yet has many
> members, and all the members of the body,
> though they are many, are one body, so also is
> Christ. For by one Spirit we were all baptized
> into one body, whether Jews or Greeks, whether
> slaves or free, and we were all made to drink of
> one Spirit.

There is one Lord who died and paid the penalty of our sins, conquered death, and purchased our salvation. In Him, we place our faith as our Savior and Lord and declare it publicly through baptism.

The One who initiated all of this is the one God and Father who is above all (authority), through all (present in every part of the process), and in all (united to the Spirit and the Son and to the provision of salvation). All of this is done in infinite unity within the Godhead that powerfully overwhelms the forces and works of darkness and evil.

Brooke Foss Westcott rightly observes, "Perhaps the most dangerous symptom in popular theology is the neglect of the doctrine of God in His unity." This Ephesians passage also indicates that this unity is a reality because the Father is "above all," meaning He's responsible, initiating, overseeing, and ruling. The Holy Spirit and Jesus are powerfully and joyfully submitting to the Father's oversight and initiative. There is no unity without clear authority, and here they both exist to an infinite degree. This is our hope for unity in our homes and in our churches.

In Ephesians 3:14-21, the teaching about the Father's authority and the submission of Jesus and the Holy Spirit to that authority is more indirect and by implication, but it's still present and clear. Paul recognizes the difficulty we have as humans in this earthly existence to connect to an unseen God and His involvement in our lives. He therefore prays on behalf of the Ephesians to the Father about this problem that we all face:

> For this reason I bow my knees before the Father, from whom every family in heaven and on earth derives its name, that He would grant you, according to the riches of His glory, to be strengthened with power through His Spirit in the inner man, so that Christ may dwell in your hearts through faith; and that you, being rooted and grounded in love, may be able to comprehend with all the saints what is the breadth and length and height and depth, and to know the love of Christ which surpasses knowledge, that you may be filled up to all the fullness of God.
>
> Now to Him who is able to do far more abundantly beyond all that we ask or think, according to the power that works within us, to Him be the glory in the church and in Christ Jesus to all generations forever and ever. Amen.

The authority within the Godhead is seen in several important ways:

1. **Paul prays to the Father.** This is a recognition on his part that God the Father is the one responsible to initiate and direct the work of the triune God in ministering to our needs as His children.

2. **Paul acknowledges that "every family in heaven and on earth" derives its name from the Father.** He is the source, creator, and initiator of the concept

of a family. This concept has its eternal expression and model in the Godhead itself. It also has major implications concerning our blood families and the family of God, the Church. Westcott explains with excellent insight:

> He Who is the Father of men is also the source of fellowship and *unity* [italics added for emphasis] in all the orders of finite being. The social connections of earth and heaven derive their strength from Him; and represent under limited conditions the power of His Fatherhood . . .
>
> Every family, every society which is held together by the tie of a common head and author of its being derives that which gives it a right to the title from the one Father. From Him comes the spirit by which the members have fellowship one with another and are all brought together into a *supreme unity* [italics added for emphasis].

3. **Paul recognizes that God the Father strengthens us in the "inner man" and "with power through His Spirit."** The Father is the initiator and director. The Spirit, sent by the Father, is the agent and power accomplishing the work in us.

4. **While the Father is the initiator and director of this process, Christ is the Messiah/Son who "dwells in our hearts through faith."** It is through Jesus living and abiding in us that we can comprehend and experience the breadth, length, height, and depth of Christ's love and be filled up to all the fullness of God. I believe

it's correct to say that God the Father has initiated the love of the triune God and Jesus, the Son, is the expression and experience of that love.

This fits the many statements of Jesus referring to the Father's plan and initiative and His own response to carry out that plan. This wonderful united teamwork in the Godhead is seen in Jesus' words in John 6:37-40, 44:

> "All that the Father gives Me will come to Me, and the one who comes to Me I will certainly not cast out. For I have come down from heaven, not to do My own will, but the will of Him who sent Me. This is the will of Him who sent Me, that of all that He has given Me I lose nothing, but raise it up on the last day. For this is the will of My Father, that everyone who beholds the Son and believes in Him will have eternal life, and I Myself will raise him up on the last day . . . No one can come to Me unless the Father who sent Me draws him; and I will raise him up on the last day."

Carrying on this thought, Paul writes in 1 Corinthians 11:3:

> But I want you to understand that Christ is the head of every man, and the man is the head of a woman, and God is the head of Christ.

This passage is brief, cogent, and powerful in setting forth the whole principle of authority and submission. Charles Hodge, in his commentary on 1 Corinthians states, "That principle is, that order and subordination pervade the whole universe, and is essential to its being . . . If this concatenation be disturbed in any of its parts, ruin must be the result." Paul was instructing the Corinthian church about a cultural application of this principle regarding the wearing of a veil or head covering by women in public worship. The application is not universal or timeless, but the principle is, and Paul makes it clear in verse 10 what the heart of the issue is about: "Therefore the woman ought to have a symbol of authority on her head, because of the angels."

The Greek word *exousia* means "authority." *Thayer's* lexicon gives the fourth general meaning as "the power of rule or government," adding "the power of him whose will and commands must be submitted to by others and obeyed."

The purpose of this section from 1 Corinthians is not about submission and authority between men and women, but about how this principle works out in the relationship of Jesus to His Father; I only quote verse 10 to emphasize that the principle undergirding this discussion is about authority and submission. It is obvious that the key word in this passage is "head." Again, *Thayer's* is helpful as he defines *kephale* metaphorically as "anything supreme, chief, prominent; of persons, master, lord."

Kittel's *Theological Dictionary of the New Testament* provides more important information to this discussion. In describing the meaning and usage of this key word outside the New Testament, it indicates that there is a sequence of related meanings. The first refers to that which is "first, or supreme, at the beginning or the end"—the point, the top, the end, or the point of departure. It then adds that it also was used to refer to "what is prominent, outstanding, or determinative."

Then—and this is germane to our discussion—it asserts that when the idea of that which is determinative is linked with the point of departure, *kephale* can easily take on the sense of rule or ruler. It's my conviction that the concept of authority is clearly present in this passage if one takes the simple, clear meaning of the text. There are those who reject the whole idea of authority in all these relationships, but to get there, in my opinion, they are forced to manipulate the text to support their conclusion.

This rather complicated debate is dealt with by Thomas R. Schreiner and Wayne Grudem in their contributions to the extensive volume entitled, *Recovering Biblical Manhood & Womanhood*. Since that debate would be a distraction to this discussion, I will refer the interested reader to that excellent work.

* * *

I also want to say that 1 Corinthians 15:24-28 is pertinent and powerful in this discussion because it rolls back the curtain of eternity and lets us see the relationship in the Godhead from that perspective.

The fifteenth chapter of 1 Corinthians is primarily about the subject of the resurrection—Christ's and ours. Nestled in this important passage of Scripture is the summary of Jesus' ministry in time and the declaration of His role and relationship with the Father:

> . . . then comes the end, when He hands over the
> kingdom to the God and Father, when He
> has abolished all rule and all authority and
> power. For He must reign until He has put all His
> enemies under His feet. The last enemy that will
> be abolished is death. FOR HE HAS PUT ALL THINGS IN
> SUBJECTION UNDER HIS FEET. But when He says, "All
> things are put in subjection," it is evident that
> He is excepted who put all things in subjection to
> Him. When all things are subjected to Him, then
> the Son Himself also will be subjected to the One
> who subjected all things to Him, so that God may
> be all in all.

This passage corresponds to everything God says about His Son in terms of honor and position. In Psalm 2:7-9, the eternal Son of God proclaims:

> "I will surely tell of the decree of the LORD;
> He said to Me, 'You are My Son,
> Today I have begotten You.
>
> 'Ask of Me, and I will surely give the nations as Your inheritance,
> And the very ends of the earth as your possession.
>
> 'You shall break them with a rod of iron,
> You shall shatter them like earthenware.'"

This theme is referred to by Paul in Philippians 2:9-11:

> For this reason also, God highly exalted Him, and bestowed on Him the name which is above every name, so that at the name of Jesus EVERY KNEE WILL BOW of those who are in heaven and on earth and under the earth, and that every tongue will confess that Jesus Christ is Lord, to the glory of God the Father.

The passage in 1 Corinthians tells us several important things about Jesus Christ, the Son of God. First, at the end of time Jesus will deliver the kingdom He has won to the God and Father. This action clearly implies that God and Father is the person in authority and is "determinative" in every issue and process in heaven and on earth, and it also clearly indicates that Jesus the Son submits Himself voluntarily to His Father.

Second, this passage teaches that Jesus has "abolished all rule and all authority and power." The subject of authority is dominant in this passage and is the subject and the context of the final statements of this section of Scripture.

Third, because this entire chapter is about the resurrection, Jesus' victory over every enemy includes death, the "last enemy that will be abolished." The only exception to Jesus' total vanquishing of all authority is the Father who initiated and determined this process.

Fourth, when this process has come to completion, Jesus Himself, the victor over all authority and power, will "be subjected to the One who subjected all things to Him, so that God may be all in all." This part of the submission of Christ to the Father is connected to the completion of His work of redemption and the subduing of all principalities, powers, rulers, and authorities.

As Hodge summarizes, "The passage does not teach us the design of redemption, but what is to happen when the redemption of God's people is accomplished. Then the Messianic reign is to cease, and God is to rule supreme over a universe reduced to order, the people of God being saved, and the finally impenitent shut up with Satan and his angels in the prison of despair."

In my research, I've found that an interpretation of this passage must be rejected—the notion that Jesus' submission to His Father was only as the Son of Man here on the earth. This interpretation is based on the fear that submission requires inferiority, and that, if true, would destroy the co-equal status of the Son. But as we have already discussed, submission does *not* require inferiority. This distortion has confused some biblical commentators. Jesus Christ, the Son of God, is equal to the Father ontologically—that is, in essence, substance, and personhood. He is subject or subordinate to the Father in role and function and administration. This same interpretation has also failed to acknowledge that the subordination of the Son to the Father is inherent in His nature as Son. This is the order and arrangement of how the equal members of the Trinity relate to each other as they function in their distinct roles, responsibilities, and personalities. Hodge again is helpful when he writes:

Paul is speaking simply of the continuance of the mediatorial dominion of Christ over the universe. That dominion was given to Him for a specific purpose; when that purpose is accomplished, He will give it up, and God, instead of reigning through Christ, will be recognized as the immediate sovereign of the universe; His co-equal, co-eternal Son clothed in our nature, being, as the everlasting head of the redeemed, officially subordinate to Him.

It's probably true that some of the difficulty we have in understanding how the Son can be equal with the Father and subordinate at the same time is the same difficulty God's people have had in understanding the Trinity and the two natures of Christ, the *Theanthropos* (God-man).

However, clarity on this issue is of the greatest importance in understanding how God's authority is expressed in this world. This is true not only concerning the Godhead, but also in all its human, this-worldly applications. A right understanding of this spiritual principle of authority is essential to our ability to live out the purposes and ways of God for us in our homes, our work places, our churches, our nation, and our world.

GODLY AUTHORITY AS IT APPLIES TO THE WORLD

As in every aspect of our lives, the understanding and application of godly authority in the world is difficult, complicated, and, at times, filled with anguish and suffering.

That said, we are incredibly blessed as God's people to have His sure and eternal Word in the Scriptures. As in everything in our lives, God's Word is right, true, and powerful to help us understand and obey His ways. In considering how God's authority works out in our lives here on this earth, I will look at the two key areas in which this process manifests itself: work and government.

Godly Authority in Our Work

To begin with, it will be important for you to understand God's view of work. Work is not intended by God to be a "necessary evil." Work was part of God's creative purpose for us through Adam and Eve before the Fall.

Work is a way for us to participate with God in bringing order, beauty, and purpose to the world in which we live, and thus to our lives. Work is a godly activity because it reflects God's activity. The Psalmist expresses deep emotion and delight when he sings:

> O Lord, how many are Your works,
> In wisdom You have made them all;
> The earth is full of Your possessions.
>
> —Psalm 104:24

Furthermore, God takes great delight in His works. No less than six times God reflects on His creative work and "saw that it was good" in the first chapter of Genesis. This delight is expressed by God in Genesis 1:31:

> And God saw all that He had made, and behold, it
> was very good.

The Almighty is referred to multiple times in the Scriptures as the God who made the world and all things in it. Since God has obviously enjoyed His work and continues to enjoy it, it makes sense that He would want us to participate with Him and enjoy our work as well.

Some thirty-odd years ago, our family of four adult children and two spouses decided to build a mountain home together. I can still remember one day, while working on placing the 2x12 rafters, thinking about how hard it was to construct this building well. This led me into another thought: how small our project was compared to the vastness of God's perfect work of creation. My last thought was how exciting it was to build this home as an act of participating with God in creating and building something. I'm convinced that this is how we need to view all our work.

After the Fall, Adam had to work while experiencing the severe consequence of his disobedience. God's solemn words to him were these:

> "Cursed is the ground because of you;
> In toil you will eat of it
> All the days of your life.
> Both thorns and thistles it shall grow for you;
> And you will eat the plants of the field;
> By the sweat of your face
> You will eat bread."
>
> —Genesis 3:17b-19a

While there was a significant element of consequence in Adam's expulsion from the Garden of Eden and the curse on the ground and the toil he could expect, God's mercy was also on display. God's banishment of Adam and Eve happened because God did not want them to eat of the tree of life and live forever in this now death-infected world. His plan of redemption from sin, death, and a world soaking in corruption was activated, which would include the sending and giving of His "only begotten Son."

In other words, God's grace began to operate the moment death took over. His grace will win as Paul powerfully indicates in Romans 8:18-39. The point I want to make is that in a fallen world, the expulsion from the Garden and, by extension, the difficulty attached to work, are both an expression of God's mercy as well as a severe consequence of our disobedience.

There is no love in leaving us in this broken world of sickness, evil, death, and destruction forever. Our work, which isn't easy, is a protection for us in that work limits our opportunities to participate in the misery and evil of this world. Even though difficult, the consequence of work gives us purpose and fulfillment as well as meaning to our lives.

This also keeps us from having too much time to reflect on the evil we brought into this world and the misery it creates. Overwhelming depression, if too free to reflect, would envelop us and destroy any hope for living. As it is, we still battle turmoil and depression even though we may be working regularly and somewhat successfully.

The conclusion of these depressing thoughts is that even in this fallen world work is a good thing. What lifts our spirits and brings significant joy and peace into our lives is that Jesus Christ can deliver us from the evil of this world and bring us into His kingdom of light and life. In addition, He guarantees our hope for an eternal future with Him, where all evil, death, sickness, and destruction will be gone. But work is still a necessary discipline that God has given us to limit the effects of evil and our participation in it.

So how does submission to authority impact the process of work and our participation in it? A great place to start is 1 Peter 2:18-19, which I shared in Chapter 1, but I want to revisit this important passage of Scripture with a new emphasis:

> Servants, be submissive to your masters with all
> respect, not only to those who are good and gentle,
> but also to those who are unreasonable. For this
> finds favor, if for the sake of conscience toward
> God, a person bears up under sorrows when suf-
> fering unjustly.

This passage about slaves and masters can be applied to employees and employers today. The general consensus among historians is that in the Roman Empire, slavery was the major source of workers and laborers. Regardless of whether this is totally true or not, it's obvious that when Peter wrote this letter, slaves did work for their masters.

The Greek word *upotasso* in the middle voice clearly means to subject one's self, to obey. This is the most common word used in the New Testament to refer to the relationship of one under the authority of another. In this passage, the principle of submission to authority (in this case, that of slaves to masters) is extremely important to God. He makes it clear that obedience to this principle is even more important than being treated with justice and fairness.

The reason for this, Peter explains, is because if you suffer unjustly for doing what is right, you are doing it "for the sake of conscience toward God." That is, this is what God has commanded you to do. This means your fear of God and your resulting obedience is more important than your personal experience of justice and pleasantness, and when you do that, "this finds favor [with God]."

This would appear to mean that you please God when you do

what He says. While this is always true, there may be an additional truth that's expressed in the Greek text because the word *finds* is not in the original text.

But first, let me start with the word translated into *favor* from the Greek, which is *karis. Thayer's* provides helpful insight, stating that the New Testament writers use of *karis* predominantly expresses a type of "kindness by which God bestows favors even upon the ill-deserving, and grants to sinners the pardon of their offenses, and bids them accept of eternal salvation through Christ."

Given the importance God has placed on the principle of submission to authority in this passage, it's clear to me that this stated usage of *karis* (or grace) is a better way to translate the text. Instead of "this finds favor with God," the translation should be, "this is grace with God."

I don't think it would be a stretch to interpret this to mean that when we suffer unjustly after submitting to those in authority over us, we participate with God in revealing His grace to this undeserving person. Expressing grace *with* God to someone who does not deserve it is more effective in convicting a sinful, unreasonable, unjust employer than fighting for justice. That employer is brought face to face with something more powerful than his or her selfishness and sinfulness.

This is the power of submission.

* * *

Another informative passage of Scripture is found in Ephesians 6:5-8 from Paul:

> Slaves, be obedient to those who are your masters
> according to the flesh, with fear and trembling,
> in the sincerity of your heart, as to Christ; not by
> way of eyeservice, as men-pleasers, but as slaves

of Christ, doing the will of God from the heart.
With good will render service, as to the Lord, and
not to men, knowing that whatever good thing
each one does, this he will receive back from the
Lord, whether slave or free.

To begin with, the word for *obey* is different than the word used in 1 Peter 2:18, which is translated "be submissive to." The Greek word *upakouo* is translated by *Thayer's* in this way: "to hearken to a command, that is to obey, to be obedient unto, to submit to."

My understanding of these two words is that *upotasso* or "to submit to" is a more general meaning of putting yourself into a submissive position to those in authority, while *upakouo*, which means "to obey," is the specific carrying out of a command. Both are clear, strong terms regarding the concept of submission to authority.

Paul adds that this obedience should be accompanied by fear and trembling, which are descriptive words that add a high level of intensity to the command "to obey."

The word for *fear* has the connotation of dread or terror. The word for *trembling* is a reference to what the fear produces in one's physical body. While a resultant meaning of fear is that of reverence and respect, it's my conviction that this element of dread or terror needs to be present. I say this because the word for *trembling* intensifies this concept of fear and also implies that we understand the gravity of evil and God's relentless opposition and judgment of evil.

Even though in Christ we shouldn't fear God's condemnation and judgment, we still need to acknowledge the horrendous reality of evil and God's holy stand against it. This ongoing cosmic conflict should find more than the response of reverence and respect in our souls, especially because these two concepts are so diluted in our human society. It's my observation that the majority of society's problems, other than economic issues, stem from people having a lack of understanding of and submission to those in authority over them.

Many years ago, I listened to a man named Keith W. Phillips talk about training inner city youth to be good employees. His formula was simple: "Show up, show up on time, and do exactly what they tell you." In his strongly encouraging and highly practical book, *Out of Ashes,* Phillips tells the story of James, one of the young people he helped get a job bussing tables at a Sizzler restaurant.

Less than two hours after James' employment started, he showed up back in the projects, his head hanging low. He looked at Phillips and said, "I quit."

"Why?" he asked.

"The boss was mean. He told me to pick up all these dirty dishes, clean up every table in the restaurant, and then wash the dirty floor in the kitchen. I didn't sign up for that, man."

It was clear that James had had enough. After all, any guy on the street who put up with such orders without resistance would be walked all over. When that happened to James, he turned and slugged the boss square in the mouth, tore off his apron, and walked out of that restaurant for good, which ended his first venture in employment.

Admittedly, most job hires do not include this kind of drama, but it's my conviction that most work problems, other than economic, involve some degree of resistance to authority. The conflict may be subtler or become "passive aggressive," but it usually boils down to the individual not wanting anyone to tell him or her what to do.

Paul's words to slaves about the importance of fearful and respectful obedience are powerfully applicable to employees. When a person sincerely and even joyfully embraces his position of submission to authority, based on his healthy fear of God, it frees him to understand and experience Paul's next principle about work.

The principle to keep in mind is this: Don't do your work to look good or even to please your boss. Instead, reach way higher and act as a slave of Christ, which causes you to "[do] the will of God from the heart."

Submission and obedience to authority is all about God and His will for us. We are to "render service, as to the Lord, and not to men." And Paul makes it clear that in doing so we will be doing good things and good works. This in turn releases God's blessings because we "will receive back from the Lord."

What Paul outlines here is a tremendous, positive chain of consequences. Nothing is any better in life than knowing that you're doing God's will and serving Him. This transforms work into something sacred and eternally significant, but it begins with a submissive spirit and an obedient heart. When it comes to the power of submission, I think it would be fair to say that there's no better way to succeed and advance in one's vocation than to follow these godly, freeing, and effective biblical principles.

The workplace is not a one-way street, however. Paul also indicates in his writings that masters/employers have a major responsibility in fitting in with God's truths about authority, starting with granting "your slaves justice and fairness." The reason for this, Paul explains, is that they "have a Master in heaven" (Colossians 4:1).

This points us to an intense revealing of God's view of masters/employers in James 5:4:

> Behold, the pay of the laborers who mowed your
> fields, and which has been withheld by you, cries
> out against you; and the outcry of those who did
> the harvesting has reached the ears of the Lord of
> Sabaoth.

James is no doubt expositing God's truth as spoken in Leviticus 19:13b:

> "The wages of a hired man are not to remain with you all night until morning."

This important truth is expanded in Deuteronomy 24:14-15:

> "You shall not oppress a hired servant who is poor and needy, whether he is one of your countrymen or one of your aliens who is in your land in your towns. You shall give him his wages on his day before the sun sets, for he is poor and sets his heart on it; so that he will not cry against you to the LORD and it become sin in you."

Work is obviously an important concern of our God, the Lord of hosts, and the core principle involved in working is all about the issue of authority. Employees are to have a submissive spirit and an obedient heart. Employers are to exercise their authority with "justice and fairness."

I wonder how following this balanced truth would impact our labor and management issues in our country. I think it would certainly help and create a better work environment. That said, God's Word should challenge us to understand how these truths can make our work fulfilling, exciting, and godly.

God's Authority in Our Government

The first two verses of Romans 13 were considered at the beginning of this book, and now I want to look closer at verses 3-7, which are an application of verses 1 and 2 and our relationship to government authority. Let's start with a closer look at Romans 13:3-7:

For rulers are not a cause of fear for good behavior, but for evil. Do you want to have no fear of authority? Do what is good and you will have praise from the same, for it is a minister of God to you for good. But if you do what is evil, be afraid; for it does not bear the sword for nothing; for it is a minister of God, an avenger who brings wrath on the one who practices evil.

Therefore it is necessary to be in subjection, not only because of wrath, but also for conscience' sake. For because of this you also pay taxes, for rulers are servants of God, devoting themselves to this very thing. Render to all what is due them: tax to whom tax is due; custom to whom custom: fear to whom fear; honor to whom honor.

Paul describes God's perspective on human government, which is for the purpose of restraining evil by "[bringing] wrath" on those who practice it. Government is also seen as "a minister of God" for our "good."

God is very concerned about order in society, and He sees human governments carrying out that order. Our response to that authority is to be in subjection, which allows us to support God's wrath against evil. Paul also indicates that our submission to governmental authority is for "conscience' sake." This is because it's God's will for us to be submissive to governmental authority. To obey God's will brings a quiet and peaceful conscience. Paul's question, "Do you want to have no fear of authority?" suggests that a posture of not fearing authority is a manifestation of great foolishness that goes against how God orders this universe, including human society.

An interesting and crucial issue raised by Paul's teaching lies in the fact that the Roman government, under which Paul and the early Christians lived, was far from godly. Even though Rome had a sophisticated commitment to the rule of law at the time, no one is ever going to claim that Roman authority was known for its goodness and righteousness. That said, Rome actually had a more humane expression of slavery than our Southern states did prior to the Civil War. In Paul's time, it was possible for slaves to earn or buy their own freedom.

On the other hand, living under Roman rule was no picnic two thousand years ago. Its rulers were known for their arrogance, licentiousness, cruelty, and godlessness. Even though the Romans worshipped many deities, the true and living God was not one of them. They also were best known for conquering other nations to benefit their economy and satisfy their blood lust.

In spite of all this happening in Paul's time, God's priority of authority and order trumped any effort to overthrow this despotic government, and Paul wrote about the importance of submitting to its rulers and laws. This juxtaposition of a godless government and the submission of God's people to that government indicates how important it is to God that His authority through human agency be feared, respected, and obeyed.

This truth of Scripture raises many questions and has been central in the debates and decisions about revolutions, wars, and political processes throughout human history. More qualified people than me have wrestled with these questions, so I will leave it to the reader to seek those presentations for further thought and understanding.

In closing, though, I will say that there is almost unanimous agreement by all who have considered this issue that there is a limit as to how far our subjection to government goes. For a follower of Christ, that limit is God's will and Word. We are not asked by God to submit to an obedience that would involve disobeying Him.

He is above all government. Our total submission is to Him alone, which is also important in the home.

GODLY AUTHORITY AS IT APPLIES TO THE HOME

S ince the family is the most basic unit of human society, it's imperative to discuss God's authority in the home, which is an important prerequisite for understanding God's authority in the Church.

The biblical perspective on the home and family has been dealt with by many authors over the years, and I appreciate those who've written on this subject with amazing thoroughness and exegesis. Two of these published works that have been of significant help to me have been *Man and Woman in Biblical Perspective,* by James B. Hurley and *Recovering Biblical Manhood & Womanhood*, edited by John Piper and Wayne Grudem.

These books honor Scripture over culture and highlight the authority issue in the home as well as the absolute equality of men and women in terms of value, importance, and relationship to God. The authors also unpack the leadership and authority of men in the family and in the Church.

Authority in God's kingdom does not include any notion of superiority or inferiority. In fact, it's the confusion of these two that seems to be the driving presupposition of contemporary Christian feminists. This is why, after discussing the Godhead in relationship to authority in previous chapters, I want to pivot and consider the issue of godly authority in the family in relation to the husband and the wife, and secondly, in terms of parents and children.

Godly Authority as It Relates to Husband and Wife

L et's begin by going back to the beginning of creation and viewing what God says and does. I begin in Genesis 1:26-27:

> Then God said, "Let Us make man in Our image,
> according to Our likeness; and let them rule over
> the fish of the sea and over the birds of the sky
> and over the cattle and over the earth, and over
> every creeping thing that creeps on the earth." God
> created man in His own image, in the image of God
> He created him; male and female He created them.

Note several important truths about men and women that are highlighted in this passage. First, they are both made in the image of God. This, by inference, means that both male and female are necessary to express and manifest the image of God in humanity. This refers to their equality in value, importance, essence, and relationship to God.

This defined equality between male and female is what Paul refers to in Galatians 3:28 as he declares:

> There is neither Jew nor Greek, there is neither
> slave nor free man, there is neither male nor
> female; for you are all one in Christ Jesus.

Second, men and women are both given the assignment to rule over God's creation. Their purpose in life is to participate with Him in His purposes and plans and to do His will. Third, they are to do this in unity.

The interplay between the pronouns "him" and "them" would indicate both the unity and the diversity of male and female, which leads me to relate the fourth important truth, which is: male and female He created them. They are not the same. There is clear emphasis and distinction about male and female.

When you read Genesis 2, you'll see another description of God's creation that fills in several details not included in the first chapter, namely the differences between male and female.

The first thing I want to point out is that God created Adam, the male, first, in verse 7, and then He "took the man and put him into the garden of Eden to cultivate it and keep it."

God, still having not created Eve, next instructed Adam about his relationship of obedience and trust in Genesis 2:16-17:

> The LORD GOD commanded the man, saying, "From any tree of the garden you may eat freely; but from the tree of the knowledge of good and evil you shall not eat, for in the day that you eat from it you will surely die."

God then expands the man's responsibilities in God's creation when He brings to him "every beast of the field and every bird of the sky . . . to see what he would call them, and whatever the man called a living creature, that was its name" (2:19b).

Adam took on this responsibility and "gave names to all the cattle and to the birds of the sky, and to every beast of the field" (2:20b), but God was not finished with His creation activity. In His wisdom and purpose, He planned that man should not live in isolation. He understood that Adam was not complete without a helper:

> Then the LORD GOD said, "It is not good for the man to be alone; I will make him a helper suitable [literally meaning "corresponding to"] for him."
> —Genesis 2:18

This "helper" is so important to God that He clearly describes the process of His provision for Adam, which is the completion of His creative work:

So the LORD GOD caused a deep sleep to fall upon
the man, and he slept; then He took one of his
ribs and closed up the flesh at that place. The
LORD God fashioned into a woman the rib which
He had taken from the man, and brought her to
the man.

—Genesis 2:21-22

It's important to note that God's assignment to participate with Him in His purpose for His creation included the command recorded in the first chapter: "Be fruitful and multiply, and fill the earth, and subdue it."

This description from God is the establishment of male and female in their sexuality.

The eternal importance of this responsibility and privilege of being part of God's creation is referred to by Paul in his discourse with the philosophers in Athens. In Acts 17:26-28a, he declared to them:

". . . and He made from one man every nation
of mankind to live on all the face of the earth,
having determined their appointed times and the
boundaries of their habitation, that they would
seek God, if perhaps they might grope for Him
and find Him, though He is not far from each one
of us; for in Him we live and move and exist . . ."

There are two important truths to glean from this consideration of God's creation of mankind. First, it's clear that to fulfill God's purposes, the creation of both man and woman—male and female—are equally necessary to accomplish these purposes. This is true in at least two ways:

- to manifest the image of God

- complete the work He has called us as humans to do

Furthermore, it's clear that there are some differences as to how God created and assigned the different genders to man and woman, as described before. So what do these differences indicate? How should we interpret them, especially in light of this discussion on authority?

The answer, I firmly believe after a lifelong study of this topic, is that leadership and authority in the home and in the Church have been assigned to men. Consider these six points:

1. When God's created humanity, He created the man first.

2. He formed the man directly from the "dust from the ground, and breathed into his nostrils the breath of life; and man became a living being" (Gen. 2:7b). Once He determined that Adam needed a helper, He then "built" a woman from the rib of the man.

3. God assigned man, without the woman being present, to "cultivate" and "keep" the garden where He had placed him (see verse 15).

4. God, before He created the woman, instituted humanity's relationship with its Creator by establishing moral and spiritual accountability stemming from dependence upon and obedience to the Creator. This He did by giving Adam the freedom to eat of every tree in the garden except one: the tree of the knowledge of good and evil.

5. Before God created the woman, He assigned Adam to name "all the cattle, and to the birds of the sky,

and to every beast of the field" (see verse 20). God Himself brought all these living creatures to Adam, which he named.

6. After preparing Adam to see his need for a partner and helper, "the LORD GOD said, 'It is not good for the man to be alone; I will make him a helper suitable [or corresponding] for him'" (verse 18b). These six differences in the way God created the man as opposed to how, when, and why He created the woman do not indicate that God's creation of the woman was an afterthought. Nor do they indicate any inferiority inherent in the woman. What they do indicate is that God established a pattern of order and function in the way He brought about a man and a woman and how they are to relate to each other.

The foundational and underlying principle that infuses meaning to this pattern of order and function is the principle of authority. What's important to remember here is that authority in all relationships has to do with who should initiate in the relationship, who is determinative, and who is ultimately responsible for what happens to the relationship.

* * *

This would be a good time to look at what New Testament teaching has to say about the roles of the sexes. I'll start with 1 Corinthians 11:3-12, keeping the verse numbers:

> 3 But I want you to understand that Christ is the head of every man, and the man is the head of a woman, and God is the head of Christ. 4 Every man who has something on his head while

praying or prophesying disgraces his head. [5] But every woman who has her head uncovered while praying or prophesying disgraces her head, for she is one and the same as the woman whose head is shaved. [6] For if a woman does not cover her head, let her also have her hair cut off; but if it is disgraceful for a woman to have her hair cut off or her head shaved, let her cover her head. [7] For a man ought not to have his head covered, since he is the image and glory of God; but the woman is the glory of man. [8] For man does not originate from woman, but woman from man; [9] for indeed man was not created for the woman's sake, but woman for the man's sake. [10] Therefore the woman ought to have a symbol of authority on her head, because of the angels. [11] However, in the Lord, neither is woman independent of man, nor is man independent of woman. [12] For as the woman originates from the man, so also the man has his birth through the woman; and all things originate from God.

Note that verse 3 asserts "Christ is the head of every man, and the man is the head of a woman, and God is the head of Christ." This passage, which has everything to do with authority, is clear from the usage of the word "head" in verse 3. It's also clear that the word *authority* appears in verse 10 where it says, "Therefore the woman ought to have a symbol of authority on her head, because of the angels."

The phrase, "because of the angels" highlights the importance of the principle of authority as it flows from God the Father into the various relationships of the Godhead and of His creation. The angels operate with joy under this principle and are well aware of the consequences of violating this tenet. It's worth quoting British theologian Charles Hodge again when he makes this comment on verse 3:

> That principle is, that order and subordination
> pervade the whole universe, and is essential to its
> being . . . If this concatenation be disturbed in any
> of its parts, ruin must be the result.

In the context of authority, this principle becomes the most natural interpretation to understand that God was preparing the man to be in that place of authority and to be determinative in his relationship to the woman. This He did by creating the man first.

Paul used this act to support his teaching that the man is the head of a woman as seen in 1 Corinthians 11:8, when he wrote, "For man does not originate from woman, but woman from man."

Paul did the same in his first pastoral letter to Timothy when he asserted that a woman should not "teach or exercise authority over a man" (1 Timothy 2:12b). He based this on his exposition of Genesis 2 where Adam was created first. Paul believed that the wife's role of submission to her husband was inherent in creation: Adam was created first, and then Eve. End of argument.

New Testament scholar Douglas Moo writes in *Recovering Biblical Manhood & Womanhood*:

> Paul emphasizes that man was created "first,
> then" Eve; the temporal sequence is strongly
> marked (*protos,* "first," and *eita,* "then"). What is
> the point of this statement? Both the logic of this
> passage and the parallel in 1 Corinthians 11:3-10
> make this clear: for Paul, the man's priority in the
> order of creation is indicative of the headship that
> man is to have over woman. The woman being

created after man, as his helper, shows the position of submission that God intended as inherent in the woman's relation to the man.

James B. Hurley, in his book *Man and Woman in Biblical Perspective*, points out the principle of primogeniture (being first born) in both the Old and New Testaments, concluding, "Paul's appeal to the prior formation of Adam is an assertion that Adam's status as the oldest carried with it the leadership appropriate to a first-born son." The extension of this primogeniture principle is that Adam was formed directly by God, while Eve was built indirectly from Adam as God used his rib as the source material. This is what Paul was referring to 1 Corinthians 11:8 when he explains, "For man does not originate from woman, but woman from man."

The apostle uses this as an explanation of why the man is "the image and glory of God; but the woman is the glory of man" (see verse 7). The meaning of Paul's provocative statement only makes sense in the context of verse 3, where the man is in the position of authority as the head over the woman.

Regarding the issue of authority, the man is the image and glory of God the Father who "is the head of Christ" (see verse 3). The issue at hand—authority—is affirmed in verse 10: "Therefore the woman ought to have a symbol of authority on her head, because of the angels."

Paul is taking the *principle* of authority stated in verse 3 and directing the *application* of the principle to a woman covering her head in the public worship, which is the cultural way of her acknowledging her husband as her head.

* * *

Another key concept in establishing the man as the leader in a place of authority over the woman is God's specific assignments to the man *before* He "builds" the woman from the rib of the man. There were three specific assignments of responsibility that God gave to Adam before He created Eve to be his helper in those assignments:

- **The first assignment is described in Genesis 2:15: "Then the LORD God took the man and put him into the garden of Eden to cultivate it and keep it."**

  This first assignment has to do with man's role in caring for this earth and ruling over it as described in Genesis 1:26-28. In Genesis 1, it's evident that God intends for the woman to be part of this assignment. In Genesis 2, it's revealed that the man bears the first and ultimate responsibility for this assignment because it was given to him first and before Eve was on the scene.

- **The second assignment has to do with the presence and problem of evil that somehow and somewhere is present even in this "perfect" creation.**

  This is explained by God in Genesis 2:16-17: "The LORD GOD commanded the man, saying, 'From any tree of the garden you may eat freely; but from the tree of the knowledge of good and evil you shall not eat, for in the day that you eat from it you will surely die.'"

  This is an introduction to the major theme of God's revelation of Himself: His holiness. God's holiness is an attribute that describes His relationship to evil. He is set apart from it (Habakkuk 1:13); He is never infected or contaminated by it (1 John 1:5); He is never tempted by it (James 1:13); He is in total control of it (Job 1:6-12); He is committed to empowering His creation, including mankind, to win over it (Matthew 6:13); and He will some glorious day destroy it (Revelation 20:1-21:8).

God's command to Adam is to not have anything to do with evil, even the knowledge of it. In other words, the core principle of staying away from evil is to obey God's command.

This was a test of obedience, but Adam's failure to obey God resulted in the entire human race being plunged into sin and living under the control of the evil one (Romans 5:12; Ephesians 2:1-3). God's relentless purpose to overcome evil on our behalf involved sending His only begotten Son, Jesus, into this now death-infected world to destroy death and evil through the perfect, infinite sacrifice of His life on the cross of Calvary (John 3:16; Ephesians 2:4-9).

- **The third assignment given to Adam before Eve was created was that of naming all the animals.** This demanding process is summarized for us in Genesis 2:20 after God had "brought them to the man to see what he would call them" (see verse 19b). What happened next is described in verse 20a: "The man gave names to all the cattle, and to the birds of the sky, and to every beast of the field."

Once again, Adam receiving this assignment from God puts him in the place of primary responsibility for this work. The absence of Eve highlights his responsibility and its corresponding authority. Having the primary responsibility is a major part of ascribing authority to the man.

But here's another point: it's this responsibility that awakens the man to realize that he needs help, and this directive also reveals that God does not intend the man to do his work for God on his own. God had said previously in Genesis 2:18b that "It is not good for the man to be alone; I will make him a helper suitable [corresponding] for him."

Understand here that God is not saying a woman is inferior or an afterthought. What He is saying is that the man who leads cannot lead without the woman who helps and follows. They are mutually dependent and equally important to accomplish the work and purposes of God.

At the same time, though, it's important to acknowledge that in this context the man is the leader and determinative; the woman is the helper and follower. John Calvin, the preeminent theologian of the Reformation, said that even though we have a "degenerate nature, some residue of divine good remains."

In his *Commentary on Genesis*, he wrote:

> On this main point hangs another, that women, being instructed in their duty of helping their husbands, should study to keep this divinely appointed order. It is also the part of men to consider what they owe in return to the other half of their kind, for the obligation of both sexes is mutual, and on this condition is the woman assigned as a help to the man, that he may fill the place of her head and leader.

Calvin is acknowledging the place of authority that this account in Genesis is giving to the man. At the same time, he is also acknowledging the equality of the sexes in value and importance to carry out the commission God gave them in Genesis 1:26-28. What Calvin has done here is reminiscent of Peter's words to husbands where he counsels and warns each of them to "show [your wife] honor as a fellow heir of the grace of life, so that your prayers will not be hindered" (1 Peter 3:7b). This equality in the midst of different roles for a man and a woman concerning authority is also spoken clearly by Paul in 1 Corinthians 11:9-12, where Paul states a woman is not independent of a man and a man is not independent of a woman.

It's been important to establish the principle of male headship in the family based on the creative order in Genesis. As I've described, that creative order has been clearly expounded upon and supported in the New Testament.

Now I'd like to turn, in the next chapter, to the support of this principle regarding the narrative of "the Fall"—Adam and Eve's decision to live independently of God.

6

MALE HEADSHIP AND AUTHORITY AS REINFORCED IN THE FALL

Having explored the relationship of man and woman in terms of authority as it is established in God's creation process and order, let's look at how this principle of authority is seen in man's decision to go his own way, disobeying God's clear command, and plunging the universe into sin, chaos, and death.

Genesis 3 contains the account of this tragic decision on the part of Eve and Adam. Following their act of disobedience, they were estranged from each other as indicated by their shame in their nakedness, prompting them to make hasty, temporary coverings with fig leaves. More importantly, they were also estranged from God, hiding themselves among the trees of the Garden when they would normally be walking with Him "in the cool of the day" (see verse 8).

There are several ways that this narrative of "the Fall" supports male leadership. First, the Lord God called to the man and asked him where he was. The man answered, "I heard the sound of You in the garden, and I was afraid because I was naked; so I hid myself" (see verse 10).

God replied, "Who told you that you were naked? Have you eaten from the tree of which I commanded you not to eat?" (see verse 11).

Notice that God was not first coming to Eve, even though she was first to eat of the forbidden fruit. He is coming to the one He put in charge of this new human enterprise, the man.

It was the man He gave the command not to eat, and it was the man He first held responsible for breaking that command.

This was made even more obvious a little later when God said to Adam, "Because you have listened to the voice of your wife, and have eaten from the tree about which I commanded you saying, 'You shall not eat from it'; cursed is the ground because of you" (see verse 17).

God was telling Adam that instead of listening to and obeying His command not to eat of the forbidden tree, he listened to the voice of his wife. This indictment tells me that a man is strongly motivated to please his wife, even to the point of displeasing God. It also tells men that God expects the man to obey Him above pleasing his wife, and to lead her in the way God has commanded the man.

All of what happened in the Garden strongly implies that God considers the man the responsible party in this relationship; which in turn strongly implies that God has given him the place of leadership on behalf of himself and his wife.

Pastor and biblical scholar Ray Ortlund affirms this, noting that in this conversation with Adam:

> God does not address Eve in this way, but God
> does issue a formal indictment of Adam before his
> sentencing. Why? Because Adam was the head,
> the finally responsible member of the partnership.
> His disobedience, not Eve's, was the pivotal factor
> in the Fall.

That Adam was considered to be the responsible party in the Fall by God is reinforced in Romans 5:12, where Paul writes, "Therefore, just as through one man sin entered into the world, and death through sin, and so death spread to all men, because all sinned."

There is a corollary thought to this revealed truth about Adam's disobedience: God expects the man to be the "first responder" to the threat of evil. Adam should have intercepted Satan's successful attempt to deceive Eve—after all, he witnessed the exchange. Instead, he didn't say a word and allowed Eve to usurp his place of authority and lead him against God's way for them.

This leads me to share two important thoughts about Eve's actions in this narrative. The first is that Eve, when confronted by God about giving Adam the forbidden fruit, replied that Satan had deceived her. This meant that she thought what Satan was suggesting would improve everything about life and God. It sounded to her like Adam's account of God's prohibition was too limiting and what Satan was saying was expansive about what God intended for her and Adam.

This is an important point because Paul refers to Eve being deceived in 1 Timothy 2:12-14 as a reason why she should not "teach or exercise authority over a man." Paul's exegesis of Genesis 3 is crucial to our interpretation of this event. In 1 Timothy, he implies that Eve's deception was a result of her assuming a role of authority that was not given to her by God. Instead of supporting her husband and respecting his authority, she took control and led him into transgression with her.

It would seem that the implication in this instance is a warning to women not to take on the leadership role that God has given to their husbands. Disobedience to that divine order brings confusion, deception, and transgression. Not only was Eve disobedient to the divine order, but she was unaware of the uniqueness and importance of how God made her.

In making the woman, God prepared her to be a helper to her husband in fulfilling God's purpose for the both of them. He also prepared her to bear children, nurture them, and love those little ones in a way that expresses an emotional sensibility that's crucial and essential to their healthy development. Paul referred to this specifically in describing his ministry to the saints in Thessalonica:

But we proved to be gentle among you, as a nursing mother tenderly cares for her own children. Having so fond an affection for you, we were well-pleased to impart to you not only the gospel of God but also our own lives, because you had become very dear to us.

—1 Thessalonians 2:7-8

The word *gentle* connects us to Peter's admonition for wives to not be overly focused on their outward appearance, "but let it be the hidden person of the heart, with the imperishable quality of a gentle and quiet spirit, which is precious in the sight of God" (1 Peter 3:4).

A gentle and quiet spirit frees a woman to be a husband lover and children lover (Titus 2:4). Both her husband and her children have great need for this emotional-nurturing content as indicated by the use of the Greek word *phileo*—a type of love that is more connected to "sense and emotion," according to *Thayer's*. The word *phileo*, translated as "tenderly cares," means to warm, keep warm, to cherish with tender love, or to foster with tender care—descriptions that communicate how God has "wired" women to bring this crucial nurturing, sensitive, compassionate, and emotional love to our world, beginning with their husbands and children.

Our families, and society at large in this 21ˢᵗ century, are severely lacking and suffering because many of our women have forsaken this God-ordained responsibility and privilege. The importance of this awareness of the woman's God-infused inclination to nurture lies in the implication that nurturing and relating can interfere with her awareness of the need to stand against evil and false teaching. This is precisely what happened in her conversation with Satan in the Garden.

It's not that she's unable to stand against evil at all, but rather

God does not want her to bear the *primary* responsibility in this battle. God wants her to support her husband in the battle because he is the one who should take on this primary responsibility—one that God has given to him.

There is one other support of male headship from the Genesis account of the Fall when God spoke to Eve about the consequences of her eating of the forbidden tree and giving it to her husband:

> "I will greatly multiply
> Your pain in childbirth,
> In pain you will bring forth children;
> Yet your desire will be for your husband,
> And he will rule over you."
>
> —Genesis 3:16b

It is clear what God is saying about the first part of Eve's consequences, but the second part seems more difficult to comprehend. Particularly, what does "your desire will be for your husband" mean?

Keep in mind that the context of these consequences, for Eve as well as Adam, was definitely negative. Therefore, each one was communicating a negative result of Eve's deception. This meant that her desire for her husband was somehow negative, and his ruling over her was somehow negative.

There's a phrase in Genesis 4:6-7 where God was speaking to Cain about his anger that his offering was unacceptable, and it goes like this: "Then the LORD said to Cain, 'Why are you angry? And why has your countenance fallen? If you do well, will not your countenance be lifted up? And if you do not do well, sin is crouching at the door; and its desire is for you, but you must master it.'"

It's quite apparent that God was saying that sin is crouching at the door (a threatening and negative posture); that its desire is to overthrow you (a threatening and negative intention); but you must master it or rule over it.

The Hebrew phrase in this passage is the same as the one used in 3:16. The words *desire* and *rule* can be used in a positive or negative context. In both 3:16 and 4:7, however, the context is negative. Therefore, the best interpretation of 3:16 is that Eve's desire for her husband was about overthrowing his leadership, which she had already done when she ate the forbidden fruit and gave it to her husband.

That said, the man's response is to rule over her in a negative way of oppression and unwanted domination. God's curse upon the woman and the man is a distortion of the loving balance of male authority and female help and submission that was established in creation before the Fall. An important implication of this truth is that God's redemption in Christ does not eliminate the relationship of authority and submission between man and woman. Rather, it restores it to its creation order prior to the Fall.

Pastor Ray Ortlund affirms:

> Therefore, while many women today need release from male domination, the liberating alternative is not female rivalry or autonomy but male headship wedded to female help. Christian redemption does not redefine creation; it restores creation, so that wives learn godly submission and husbands learn godly headship.

This emphasis on the Creation and the Fall is foundational for understanding God's intention for men and women in their relationship to the principle of authority. If this interpretation of mine is accurate, and I believe it is, then you can expect the same principle to appear in the New Testament, which is the topic of my next chapter.

THE SUPPORT IN THE NEW TESTAMENT OF MALE HEADSHIP AND AUTHORITY

Regarding the passages on male authority in the home and female submission as helper in the home, as taught in the New Testament, it will be exceedingly helpful to look closely at two passages in Scripture.

The first passage, Ephesians 5:21-31, is likely familiar to God's people in today's evangelical church because of its description of male headship and female submission in the relationship of husband and wife. Here is the entire passage with the verse numbers:

> [21] . . . and be subject to one another in the fear of Christ.
>
> [22] Wives, be subject to your own husbands, as to the Lord. [23] For the husband is the head of the wife, as Christ also is the head of the church, He Himself being the Savior of the body. [24] But as the church is subject to Christ, so also the wives ought to be to their husbands in everything.
>
> [25] Husbands, love your wives, just as Christ also loved the church and gave Himself up for her, [26] so that He might sanctify her, having cleansed her by the washing of water with the word, [27] that He might present to Himself the church in all her glory, having no spot or wrinkle or any such

thing; but that she would be holy and blameless. [28] So husbands ought also to love their own wives as their own bodies. He who loves his own wife loves himself; [29] for no one ever hated his own flesh, but nourishes and cherishes it, just as Christ also does the church, [30] because we are members of His body. [31] FOR THIS REASON A MAN SHALL LEAVE HIS FATHER AND MOTHER AND SHALL BE JOINED TO HIS WIFE, AND THE TWO SHALL BECOME ONE FLESH.

The first thing that needs to be said is how people generally interpret the phrase "be subject to one another." The interpretation is generally referred to as "mutual submission," which always ends up sounding like everybody is submissive to everybody.

I usually get that impression whenever I hear someone speaking on this subject these days. I can also tell that he or she is greatly relieved not to say the word *submission* very loudly or even clearly. It's amazing that such a freeing and beautifully integrating concept of order and function inherent in the Godhead and in all human relationships has to be whispered by the seeming majority of God's people.

That mutual submission is not based on a careful exegesis of this passage is clear for two main reasons. First, the verb in verse 22 concerning the wife's submission to her husband is not present in the Greek text but is borrowed from the participle form of the verb to submit in verse 21. This indicates that the introduction of submission to authority in verse 21 refers to some specific relationships in the body of Christ—such as wives to husbands, children to parents (in Ephesians 6:1), and slaves to masters (in Ephesians 6:5)— rather than *all* relationships.

This pattern matches the pattern in 1 Peter 2:13-3:6, where submission to authority is the foundational principle for the relationship of individuals to "every human institution." This submission to authority is spelled out in 1 Peter regarding:

- citizens to government (2:13-17)

- servants to masters (2:18-20)

- Jesus to His Father (2:21-25)

- wives to husbands (3:1-6)

This principle is supported further in Colossians 3:18-22 and Titus 2:3-5.

The second reason "mutual submission" is not a viable interpretation of this passage is because nowhere in the passage are husbands told to submit to their wives, Jesus told to submit to the Church, parents told to submit to their children, or masters told to submit to their slaves.

The same is true of all other passages where submission is referred to. Never are those *in* authority told to submit to those *under* their authority. The natural tendency of humans to resist this concept of submission to authority is greatly mitigated when we accept the clear spiritual truth that submission to authority does not imply any inferiority. I sought to make this point earlier when I said that Jesus' submission to His Father's authority did not diminish His equality with the Father.

There are several important truths regarding this principle of submission of a wife to the authority of her husband. Paul encourages wives to see their submission to their husbands as actually submission "to the Lord." This means that a wife's relationship to Jesus is the basis of her submission. If she submits to her husband's authority, she is living in obedience to Jesus Himself.

Paul reinforces this truth by asserting that "the husband is the head of the wife, as Christ also is the head of the church." This statement strongly indicates that this submission has been established by God Himself.

In Ephesians 1:18-21, Paul describes some wonderfully important things God has done for us in Christ "when He raised Him from the dead and seated Him at His right hand in the heavenly places." The apostle further explains, "And He put all things in subjection under His feet, and gave Him as head over all things to the church" (1:22).

Here in Ephesians 5, Paul applies the authority of Christ as head of the Church to be an example or model of the husband's authority over his wife. This connection to 1 Corinthians 11:3 is a clear statement of God's intentions for the principle of male headship and authority. Paul in no way equivocates on this principle when he repeats the statement in reverse in Ephesians 5:24: "But as the church is subject to Christ, so also the wives ought to be to their husbands in everything."

* * *

Paul then turns to the role of the husband and how he is to express this authority God has given him in relationship to his wife. When Paul commands, "Husbands, love your wives, just as Christ also loved the church and gave Himself up for her" in verse 25, the clear meaning is that the husband must use the authority God has given him to serve his wife by sacrificing his own needs and desires for her benefit. He is to protect her, serve her, provide for her, and lead her.

How he leads and to what end is movingly described in verses 26 and 27:

> . . . so that He might sanctify her, having cleansed
> her by the washing of water with the word, that
> He might present to Himself the church in all
> her glory, having no spot or wrinkle or any such
> thing; but that she would be holy and blameless.

This is a daunting passage of Scripture for husbands because it's the model for the way they are to love their wives. Obviously, Christ's love for the Church is of a nature and quality far beyond that of a male human for his wife, but the process and purpose of his leadership is the same in principle as that of Christ for His Church. He is to lead his wife in such a way that she will become all that God intends and desires for her as a woman of God.

This is what Adam failed to do with Eve when he submitted to her deceived and inappropriate leadership by joining her in disobeying God's clear command not to eat the fruit from the tree of the knowledge of good and evil. Both the glory of loving, godly male headship and the darkness of passively avoiding that leadership or abusing it by oppressively "lording it over" his wife make this issue of how the husband and wife are to relate to each other of utmost importance to God and to us as male and female humans.

This relationship also has major implications for society at large as we're seeing played out today. For instance, one of the driving forces behind the angry and negative component of the feminist movement is the abusive behavior of men toward women. Both in history, in the news, and in my personal pastoral experience that abuse is prevalent and devastating. These few verses in Ephesians 5 are the powerful correction to that tragic reality, not to mention being a correction to the confusion and loss resulting from the rejection of male headship in God's kingdom.

Some years ago, while I was still pastoring in a local church, a woman in our congregation came to me and reported that her husband had been involved in an adulterous affair with another woman. I met with the man and told him that he had destroyed his marriage and that he had no right to expect it to continue. I also told him that he could repent, cut off the relationship with this other woman, and ask his wife to forgive him.

While his wife may, out of obedience to God, forgive him, that did not mean she would continue to be his spouse. That would depend on the genuineness of his repentance and the rebuilding of trust with his wife. I also told him that the process could and should take a long time. While he did express some level of sorrow for his unfaithfulness and his disobedience to God, there was no clear evidence that his repentance was deep or real. Consequently, after many years, his wife divorced him. His two teenage children agreed with this separation because they also saw no genuine repentance in their father.

A few years after the divorce, this man returned to the church and asked if he could attend. The leaders of the church told him yes and encouraged him to become part of a men's accountability small group. After a couple of years in that small group, the men in the group began to believe that he was genuinely seeking God and repentance for his disobedience. His wife and children were still not convinced, however.

After a couple of more years, the kids began to believe their dad had changed and was genuinely with God and desiring to live for Him. It was some years later, twelve to be exact, that the wife was fully convinced of her husband's repentance.

During all these years, the man sincerely worked at rebuilding trust with his wife. I had the privilege of participating in their remarriage with the current pastor (I had retired several years before). This fellow has since become a godly and loving husband who loves his wife with God's help and in His presence. His wife is joyfully submitting to her husband's leadership, and together they are fellowshipping and serving God in their church and in the world.

I relate this true story as a way to show that God's ways for a man and a woman in marriage work when we obey Him. Their story also indicates how disobedience to God's ways for marriage brings devastation and sorrow to every member of the family. And, most importantly, I relate this story because it beautifully illustrates the power and wonder of God's grace in response to genuine repentance.

Jesus' simple, but profound words in Luke 24:46-47 are not just an idea or a theory, but they are an amazing reality:

> . . . and He said to them, "Thus it is written, that the Christ would suffer and rise again from the dead the third day, and that repentance for the forgiveness of sins would be proclaimed in His name to all the nations, beginning from Jerusalem."

This is what the gospel of Jesus Christ is all about.

* * *

Paul had more to say to husbands in Ephesians 5. After indicating that a man is to use his God-given authority to serve his wife, not himself, he writes that a man is to understand his position of authority in the context of a supernatural unity with his wife.

Paul quotes Moses in Genesis 2: "THE TWO SHALL BECOME ONE FLESH" (Eph. 5:31b). The spiritual implication of this mystery is that the husband is to love his wife as his own body, which is so true that "he who loves his own wife loves himself" (verse 28b). This is more than a goal for a man to seek but is a mysterious reality (verse 32), implying that a failure to love his wife will create the same loss for himself that it does for his wife. In other words, he will be as adversely affected by his failure to love her as much as he loves himself as his wife will be.

This mystery is communicated in verses 29-30 in this manner:

> . . . for no one ever hated his own flesh, but nourishes and cherishes it, just as Christ also does the church, because we are members of His body.

For a man to obey this command to love his wife in these ways supernaturally connects him to the same kind of love that Christ has for His Church. This explains the sense of loss, sadness, and fear we experience when—because of our selfishness—we have emotionally separated from our spouses over the disagreement or thoughtlessness we have communicated.

Drs. Paul and Virginia Friesen, who've written a biblical and practical book about the marriage relationship entitled *The Marriage App*, stated this:

> When we sacrificially love and put the interests of our spouse ahead of our own preferences, we benefit as well—not manipulatively, but because that is how God designed us to function in marriage. In the end, it is selfishness that kills marriages—and Christ-like sacrificial service that makes them come alive.

While the Friesens correctly include both wife and husband in this sacrificial love, I like to say to men, "Based on God's Word, no one in your family has less right to please himself than you." This is how God wants a man to use the authority He has given him to serve and "give himself up" for his wife.

There's one other important truth in this passage that I want to emphasize. When Paul writes that husbands are to love their wives as Christ loved the Church and gave Himself up for her, he is not making a suggestion. This is a command.

Sound impossible? Not really. This is something a husband is capable of doing with God's help. It's not conjuring up some feeling of love because you cannot command a feeling. Rather, it's an act of the will to obey God in the relationship. It's the kind of agape love that God has expressed for us in Christ. It's a supernatural love that only God can give us. Therefore, our only hope in fulfilling God's command to love our wives is to ask for His help and trust in His power. This is true about every command and way that God has revealed to us as men (and women) in His Word.

The power and clarity of these truths are intensified by the consistency with which they are taught throughout the Scriptures. After just having heard from Paul, the apostle to the Gentiles, I now want to turn to Peter, the apostle to the Jews. Both key leaders in the early Church proclaimed the same magnificent truth of God's order and authority in the marriage relationship.

THE POWER OF SUBMISSION

Peter, who also wrote about how God's authority is applied to marriage, explained how godly submission to God-ordained authority has an amazing power to change and redeem lives. In 1 Peter 3:1-7, Peter completes his discourse on authority—which began in 1 Peter 2:13—by focusing on the marriage relationship (verse numbers included):

> [1]In the same way, you wives, be submissive to your own husbands so that even if any of them are disobedient to the word, they may be won without a word by the behavior of their wives, [2] as they observe your chaste and respectful behavior. [3]Your adornment must not be merely external—braiding the hair, and wearing gold jewelry, or putting on dresses; [4]but let it be the hidden person of the heart, with the imperishable quality of a gentle and quiet spirit, which is precious in the sight of God. [5]For in this way in former times the holy women also, who hoped in God, used to adorn themselves, being submissive to their own husbands; [6]just as Sarah obeyed Abraham, calling him lord, and you have become her children if you do what is right without being frightened by any fear.
>
> [7]You husbands in the same way, live with your wives in an understanding way, as with someone weaker, since she is a woman; and show her

honor as a fellow heir of the grace of life, so that
your prayers will not be hindered.

This passage should look familiar since I referenced it earlier when introducing the idea of authority as a foundational issue in God's purpose in this world. Now I want to describe it in greater detail in terms of how this principle of authority is applied in the marriage relationship.

This passage from 1 Peter is not about the wife pleasing her husband as a lowly servant. It's about a woman being genuinely and fearfully obedient to the God of the universe as she displays obedience and purity in her relationship with God to her husband. She is connected to someone much bigger than him, and that is made clear in their relationship.

His awareness of this through her godly submission is what brings him face to face with her God. Peter is not telling her to fear her husband but to honor him as the leader of their home because she fears God in the highest sense of the word.

Peter then describes what this spirit of submission to God through her husband really looks like, explaining that it begins with an emphasis on the internal condition of her heart, not the outward condition of her appearance.

Peter's words, even nearly two millennia ago, are a reminder that even back then many women were more concerned with their hairdos and fashion statements than their godly relationship to their husbands. That said, the relationship of submission is not to be some external, forced behavior but should flow from a heart that is characterized by a "gentle and quiet spirit."

The word *gentle*, which can also be translated as meek or mild, is the same word used in the Beatitudes in Matthew 5:5 when Jesus said, "Blessed are the gentle, for they shall inherit the earth." It's the same word Jesus used to describe Himself in Matthew 11:29 when He said, "for I am gentle and humble in heart."

This is part of the fruit of the Spirit described in Galatians 5:23, which chronicles what it means to be a godly person and, therefore, a godly wife.

The word for *quiet* is *aesuchios*, according to *Thayer's*. This means to be *tranquil, peaceful, and not speaking, holding one's peace.* This last part may be connected to the phrase in 1 Peter 3:1 when Peter says unbelieving husbands "may be won without a word."

These adjectives for *meek* and *quiet* tell of a woman who is the opposite of someone who is worried, agitated, frustrated, or angry that things are not going the way she wants them to. These adjectives also describe a woman who's not trying to control things beyond her own responsibilities and commission from God. Instead, she is at rest in the will of a loving and sovereign God. This kind of spirit in a woman is "precious in the sight of God" (verse 4).

Barbara Sullivan, who, along with her husband, John, helped start more thirty inner-city outreaches in the Chicago area, wrote this in her honest book, *The Control Trap*:

> I myself was a very insecure, controlling person for much of my life. I am more liberated today than I have ever been—but not in the sense that the feminists espouse. My liberation has gone from fear, worry, and insecurity into a wonderful new joy as I learn to trust my heavenly Father— and trust "my world" into *His* control.

As a pastor's wife, Barbara indicates a crucial part of trusting her heavenly Father in this way:

> Women have tremendous power either for good or evil. The evil use of power is through control and domination. It is to reach out and grab the apple;

to usurp the man's leadership in the home. But women also have the power to restore what was stolen, by submission to give back the authority of headship. We women can reverse the effects of the curse on Adam and his descendants. We will set our families free from the effects of that curse and come into a oneness that is like the relationship of Christ and His Church. Now that's real power.

An Important Spiritual Connection

When Peter transitioned from the crucial inner heart characteristic of a godly wife to "the holy women . . . who hoped in God" in verse 3, their "adornment," he writes, was their submission to their husbands. He then specifically refers to Sarah as a wife who "obeyed Abraham; calling him lord" (verse 6).

I gather that most people in our 21st century society and culture cringe at these words, but Peter built on them when he continued, "and you have become her children if you do what is right without being frightened by any fear" (verse 6).

This spiritual connection of today's wives to Sarah has to do with them doing "what is right." When Peter used the term "right," he was calling on something that had been established in the past and was universally accepted as true. This "rightness" is true because it is what God has established—from the beginning when He created man as male and female. He established the male as the responsible party with the authority to carry out that responsibility alongside his wife, who God also established as his helper.

If we're going to submit our thoughts to our sovereign heavenly Father, we won't cringe at these words. Instead, we will embrace them and ask for His help to understand and obey.

Quite a few years ago, I was in a conversation with a godly missionary whose wife was on the faculty of a seminary known for its strong "egalitarian" position on gender. I do not remember how the subject of a wife's submission to her husband came up, but I do remember he was minimizing its impact with a "mutual submission" interpretation of Ephesians 5:21.

Then he argued that the Bible never asks a wife to obey her husband; that was only for children in relationship to their parents. I backed away from quarreling with him, but later I checked the Greek word used for Sarah's obedience to Abraham. It was a strong word that means "to hearken to a command, to obey, be obedient unto, submit to," according to *Thayer's*. It was also the exact same word directed at children to obey their parents in Ephesians 6:1.

I'm uncertain why otherwise godly, biblically oriented believers resist this clear biblical truth about gender in the Scriptures. What I'm convinced of, however, is that we do so at our own peril as a society, including our churches and seminaries. I can only surmise that social movements have become a higher priority than the plain and simple teaching of Scripture.

That said, I like how Peter pivots to husbands with the interesting phrase, "in the same way" in verse 7. The reason I say I like it is because it points us to something important but perhaps unclear in the words of this phrase, namely, *What "same way" is he talking about?*

I think Peter meant that a husband needs to take the authority and responsibility for leading his wife as God's commission to him in the marriage relationship. He needs to do this with the same healthy, godly fear of God that the wife has in submitting to his leadership. My experience as a pastor for some sixty years is that the vast majority of men are reluctant to be in this place of authority and leadership with their wives, especially when they understand the level of serving and sacrifice this demands.

Consider how Peter says that his leadership begins with living with his wife, meaning that he is to dwell with her. The word is a compound word of *oikos* and *sun*. *Oikos* can refer to a building, but it has strong affinity to a "house" versus any building. This means the Greek word expands to "all the persons forming one family, a household," according to *Thayer's*. The other part of this compound word is *sun*, a preposition that means "with." When used in composition, *sun* denotes "association, community, fellowship, participation," according to *Thayer's* with an additional meaning highlighting the whole concept of being "together."

Thayer's then elaborates with the idea of "several persons or things united or all in one, which is a powerful description of a healthy relationship. In this context, this compound word is referring to the whole process of coming together as husband and wife to build or "make" a home together.

This, ladies and gentlemen, is the whole concept of a marriage: dwelling together as husband and wife, male and female. The Holy Spirit wants this wonderful union to be characterized by the husband's understanding of his wife. The Greek rendering of this concept is *kata gnosin*, which means "according to knowledge."

Here are some general thoughts from *Thayer's Greek Lexicon*, beginning with *gnosis* by itself, which signifies "intelligence, understanding; moral wisdom, such as is seen in right living; in intercourse with others, wisely." A husband's understanding and knowledge of his wife has, in this passage, more to do with the fact that his wife is "someone weaker."

Peter does not explain her weakness, other than to say "since she is a woman." The lack of clarity on this "weakness" can leave this passage open to numerous interpretations, many of which are false and damaging to our understanding of male and female in a marriage relationship. Many commentators, in referring to this "someone weaker" term ("weaker vessel" in the King James Version), point out the physical differences between men and women. This is an obvious biological/anthropological truth that has been evident throughout human history because men are stronger than women. Peter could be and probably is including this biological weakness in his comment. Perhaps a more complete concept, however, has to do with a woman's weakness in terms of the issue of authority. This is the subject and context of this passage.

This would mean that a woman's submission to the authority of her husband puts her in a dependent, and therefore, "weaker" position in the marriage relationship. This interpretation is supported by Peter's words when he wrote "since she is a woman." This is not a derogatory statement about women, not at all. More likely, it could be referring to Peter's knowledge of Adam naming his God-ordained helper a "woman."

Adam's words in Genesis 2:23 are clear:

> "This is now bone of my bones,
> And flesh of my flesh;
> She shall be called Woman,
> Because she was taken out of Man."

His words acknowledge her equality with him in the essence of humanness. They also acknowledge his place of authority and thus her dependence on him. This is indicated by his naming her *woman*, meaning that she was taken out of man. This naming of her is continued in Genesis 3:20: "Now the man called his wife's name Eve, because she was the mother of all the living."

Adam was now acting in the authority God had given him to be responsible for his wife and affirming her role in the commission God had given them together to "be fruitful and multiply, and fill the earth, and subdue it" (1:28b).

Adam, in spite of their united disobedience after the Fall, responded to God's grace and forgiveness and honored Eve as the "helper" God had given him for companionship (Genesis

2:18) and completeness in their united capacity to fulfill God's purposes on this earth.

All of this defines the woman's "weakness" of dependence on the man. He is the initiator, she is the responder. He is the leader, she is the helper. This can bring uncertainty and a significant lack of control, which can foster fear, which is why the husband needs to be sensitive to this "position of weakness."

There may be another factor in Peter's referring to a woman's weakness. It has to do with how God wired her as a woman, as a wife, and as a mother. Wayne Grudem explains this as a "greater emotional sensitivity that is a great strength but also means that wives are often more likely to be hurt deeply by conflict within a marriage or by inconsiderate behavior."

When it comes to possible meanings of a woman's being weaker than a man, as indicated by Peter, a husband must have knowledge, exercise understanding, and seek wisdom, which *must* come from God Himself.

The man desperately needs God's help to be a protector, provider, and leader of his wife. Without God, men certainly can be physically abusive, emotionally demeaning, and selfishly usurp the authority God has given them for their own benefit and selfish purposes. The unloving, thoughtless, cruel, and barbaric treatment of women has dominated human history. God have mercy on us male representatives of the human race!

Peter explained positively what he meant when he wrote, "and show her honor as a fellow heir of the grace of life, so that your prayers will not be hindered" in 1 Peter 3:7. The word for *show* is *aponemo*, which means "to assign, portion out." This strongly implies an intentional act from one in authority. The verb form is a present active participle, which indicates a continuous action.

The word for *honor* is *timae*, which refers to the process of fixing a value to a person or thing and "the honor which one has by reason of the rank and state of the office which he holds," according to *Thayer's.*

In this case Peter, through the Holy Spirit, refers back to his reference to the wife as "a woman." God's order of male headship and female submission in no way weakens the high value God places on women, even though He refers to her as "someone weaker." That description does not change the fact that she is of equal value and importance in God's scheme of things. This is emphasized by Peter when he clarifies her honor "as a fellow heir of the grace of life." I believe the "grace of life" refers to everything God has purposed and accomplished for human beings in creation and salvation through His grace in Christ Jesus.

The order, in terms of roles concerning the issue of authority for male and female that was established in creation, does not in any way impact or change God's purposes in redemption for men and for women. Peter's declarations affirm and agree with Paul's passionate statement in Galatians 3:26, 28:

> For you are all sons of God through faith in Christ
> Jesus . . . There is neither Jew nor Greek, there is
> neither slave nor free man, there is neither male
> nor female; for you are all one in Christ Jesus.

It's extremely important that men understand this spiritual truth about women because God warns that any denial of this truth and the attitudes and actions resulting from this refutation will adversely affect a man's entire relationship to God. This Peter indicates when he includes the phrase, "so that your prayers will not be hindered."

In other words, if a man fails to, that will result in the hindrance of his relationship to God and his communication with Him.

9

GODLY AUTHORITY AS IT APPLIES TO PARENTS

I t's impossible to overestimate the crucial importance of author-ity as it relates to parents and children. To shed God's truth on this subject, I will spend some time considering two Old Testament passages.

Scriptural Foundations

I begin with the first family: Adam and Eve and Cain and Abel. Genesis 4:1-2 reads:

> Now the man had relations with his wife Eve,
> and she conceived and gave birth to Cain, and
> she said, "I have gotten a manchild with the help
> of the LORD." Again, she gave birth to his brother
> Abel. And Abel was a keeper of flocks, but Cain
> was a tiller of the ground.

In this passage, Eve shows the excitement of a woman who gives birth to a new life, which marks the beginning of her indis-pensable role of being fruitful, multiplying, and filling the earth. She gratefully acknowledges God's help in this wonder-filled process.

The meaning of the name Cain is "the gotten one," but Eve's excitement about bringing another life into this world must have turned somber in the naming of Abel, which means "vapor, breath" but figuratively means "unsubstantial, worthless, vanity."

This same word is used repeatedly by Solomon in the Book of Ecclesiastes.

About these two names, 19th century German theologians Karl Fredreich Keil and Franz Delitzsch helpfully explain:

> Although it cannot be supposed that Eve herself knew and uttered this name [Cain], since it was not until a later period that it was made known to man, and it really belongs to the Hebrew, which was not formed till after the division of tongues, yet it expresses the feeling of Eve on receiving this proof of the gracious help of God. But her joy was soon overcome by the discovery of the vanity of this earthly life. This is expressed in the name Abel, which was given to the second son.

John Calvin wrote in a similar vein:

> We should (in my judgment) more correctly infer, that whereas Eve had testified, in the name given to her first-born, the joy which suddenly burst upon her, and celebrated the grace of God; she afterwards, in her other offspring, returned to the recollection of the miseries of the human race.
>
> And certainly, though the new blessing of God was an occasion for no common joy; yet, on the other hand, she could not look upon a posterity devoted to so many and great evils, of which she had herself been the cause, without the most bitter grief.

This sense of despair and futility emanating from Eve is acknowledged by the Holy Spirit through the writing of Moses, the author of Genesis. That this was no exaggeration of the reality of her feelings was soon made evident in the murder of Abel by his brother Cain. The slaying of his brother indicates the depraved condition of Cain's heart, which was first brought to light by God upon the occasion of Cain's disobedient offering.

God's rejection of Cain's offering was based on the hypocrisy and rebellion in his motivation to make his sacrifice, discerned and known by God. His hypocrisy was a product of a heart that wanted to appear righteous but wasn't. God's "regard" for Abel's sacrifice was maddening to Cain because it revealed the reality of his own heart and his failure to obey God's apparent instructions concerning the meaning and giving of an offering to Him. The apostle John made this clear when he wrote:

> For this is the message which you have heard from the beginning, that we should love one another; not as Cain, who was of the evil one and slew his brother. And for what reason did he slay him? Because his deeds were evil, and his brother's were righteous.
>
> —1 John 3:11-12

The reason I'm focusing this much attention on Cain and Abel is to highlight the importance of parenting in regard to producing a righteous and godly society. Think about it: it's absolutely astonishing that within one generation of the perfection of Eden a cold-blooded murder took place. One could say that Adam and Eve's disobedience to God not only brought about immediate spiritual death and God's curse to themselves, but the ravages of that disobedience passed on to their progeny.

Our choices and actions are our own responsibility for which God will hold us accountable. In His revelation of truth through the Scriptures, however, God has made it abundantly clear that parents impact the choices and actions of their children in a significant way.

This scenario of the first family is devastatingly relevant today.

Here in America, a powerful case can be made that the major ills of our society have been spawned by irresponsible, godless, and unloving parenting.

A positive declaration by God concerning His view of parenting and redeeming humanity from the darkness of rebellion and evil is found in Genesis 18, where God announces to Abraham that his wife Sarah—past child-bearing age—was to have a son. This was the fulfillment of God's covenant with Abraham when He said to him:

> "And I will make you a great nation,
> And I will bless you,
> And make your name great;
> And so you shall be a blessing . . .
> And in you all the families of the earth will be blessed."
>
> —Genesis 12:2-3b

What God was doing was focusing on Abraham's role as a father in fulfilling God's promises and purposes for him. This He did in the context of a chaotic and wicked society. In chapter 18, God got ready to bring total destruction to two cities. Sodom and Gomorrah had become so corrupt and filled with evil that God had decided to destroy them. This terrifying scene is described this way in Genesis 19:24-25:

> Then the LORD rained on Sodom and Gomorrah
> brimstone and fire from the LORD out of heaven,
> and He overthrew those cities, and all the valley,
> and all the inhabitants of the cities, and what
> grew on the ground.

In Chapter 18, verses 17-19, God muses about His plans for destruction of these people:

The LORD said, "Shall I hide from Abraham what I am about to do, since Abraham will surely become a great and mighty nation, and in him all the nations of the earth will be blessed? For I have chosen him, so that he may command his children and his household after him to keep the way of the LORD by doing righteousness and justice, so that the LORD may bring upon Abraham what He has spoken about him."

This is an amazing revelation of God's strategy to change the world through Abraham as the leader of his home and family. Because this is nestled in between the Lord's announcement to Abraham and Sarah concerning the birth of their son and God's decision to destroy Sodom and Gomorrah, this point can easily be missed. What God is doing here is indicating how important the concept of family is to His entire purpose of redemption.

This should not surprise us since the triune God exists as a family. Paul, in Ephesians 3:14-15, points to this fact when he refers to "the Father, from whom every family in heaven and on earth derives its name." Furthermore, God's decision to commission Abraham to "command" his children and his household is a foundational principle throughout Scripture and a reminder that God intends fathers to lead their families.

This commission was not given to Sarah. Instead, it was given to Abraham. This wasn't because Sarah had no part in the raising and training of their children, but God made it clear that when it comes to the issue of authority, He expects the man to assume that role of responsibility. Sarah was to be his "helper" as God established in the bringing together of Adam and Eve in Genesis 2.

That Abraham's leadership of his family was strongly empowered by authority is indicated by God's use of the word *command*. This word has the sense of giving a charge to someone or giving an order to someone. It's the same root word used by God in Deuteronomy 6:6: "These words, which I am commanding you today, shall be on your heart." These words are a powerful delegation of authority from God, the Source of all authority, to Abraham, whose authority to command and lead his family comes directly from God Himself.

Purpose and Proper Administration of Parental Authority

While it's extremely important to establish clarity concerning authority in the parenting process—especially in our current culture where the breakdown of authority is rampant—it's equally important to make clear how that authority is to be used and for what ends.

Abraham was instructed to command his children and his household to "keep the way of the LORD by doing righteousness and justice" (Gen. 18:19b). Today, God has given a man authority in his family for a singular purpose: to lead his family in God's way of righteousness and justice.

Before a man can think about "doing righteousness and justice," though, he must understand that God is the source and standard of both virtues. They represent His way. For Abraham, this meant he had to choose to go God's way instead of his own way, which is the reverse of how Adam and Eve acted in Genesis 3. This is God's way, which is defined as doing what is right in all relationships.

This righteousness, which has the connotation of truth, is also connected in God's acts of salvation and deliverance for the repentant and acts of judgment for the unrepentant. God's way has always included justice. In fact, the *New Bible Dictionary* comes close to making these two terms—righteousness and justice—synonymous. The authors indicate that in the patriarchal stage, justice had become "conformity to . . . an accepted standard of values." They also explain that justice "comes to identify that moral standard by which God measures human conduct."

Since both terms are used, they probably are not completely synonymous, but what can be asserted is that they usually appear together and that they are both focused on what is right and wrong, good and evil, godliness and wickedness.

Here are two of numerous passages in which they appear together. I'll start with Job 37:23:

> "The Almighty—we cannot find Him;
> He is exalted in power
> And He will not do violence to justice and
> abundant righteousness."

The second is from Deuteronomy 32:4:

> "The Rock! His work is perfect,
> For all His ways are just;
> A God of faithfulness and without injustice,
> Righteous and upright is He."

God called Abraham to a life of doing what was right in His eyes and in all human relationships and activities. In this way of the Lord, Abraham was to lead his children and his household *after him* (italics mine) in Genesis 18:19, which I quoted earlier.

The words "after him" indicate that Abraham's offspring were to follow his example, but Abraham couldn't command his household in this way unless he himself was walking in that way. This same principle in parenting is highlighted in Paul's qualification for elders in 1 Timothy 3:4-5:

> He must be one who manages his own household
> well, keeping his children under control with all
> dignity (but if a man does not know how to manage
> his own household, how will he take care of the
> church of God?).

The Greek word translated as "manage" means "to be over, to superintend, preside over, to rule," according to *Thayer's*. Another sense of the word is "protecting, caring for." The writer in Kittel's *Theological Dictionary of the New Testament* explains that this word in both the Greek literature and the New Testament has a two-fold meaning of leading and caring for someone, stating, "In all these instances, however, the verb has in the New Testament the primary senses of both 'to lead' and 'to care for.'" What is crucial about this passage is that it continues God's commission to men who are fathers to take their role seriously. God expects fathers to be in the place of authority, care, and responsibility for their children.

Weldon Hardenbrook has written an impassioned article about fatherhood in *Recovering Biblical Manhood and Womanhood* entitled "Where's Dad?" Even though his article was written twenty-five years ago, it fits with the devastating trend of absent, neglectful, and distant fathers happening today:

> I humbly but firmly submit that the soul of our
> nation is in crisis in large part because American
> men have . . . abandoned their God-given role of
> fatherhood. They have discarded the notion of
> being responsible for the physical and spiritual
> well-being of those around them.

I will never forget, during my college days, a story related in our sociology class by our professor Paul Aijian. He told us of the time his father, a Presbyterian pastor, publicly resigned one Sunday morning. He told the congregation that his three boys were not walking in obedience to God's ways. Therefore, he was leaving the ministry to concentrate on calling them to repentance and God's loving ways for them.

That true story was what God used to cause me to make a similar covenant with God, namely that if my children were not walking with God, I would also leave the ministry to give myself more faithfully to their spiritual development and salvation. I made many mistakes as a father, but I believe God honored my commitment to my children and strengthened them to follow Him. These days, they are endeavoring to do the same with their children.

May we, as God's people, shout this message of male responsibility to our families from the pulpit and to our Christian educational institutions. May we also pray that our civic leaders—who have the bully pulpit—will shout the same message from the highest echelons of our governments.

And how does God see the crucial role of women in the parenting process? I'll tackle this question next.

THE ROLE OF WOMEN IN THE PARENTAL PROCESS

I t's crucially important to consider the God-given role of women as wives and mothers in the biblical parenting process, particularly as it relates to the issue of authority in the home.

Women bring two areas of contribution:

- first, in her role as helper to her husband and the father of their children

- second, in her role as providing a unique and irreplaceable emotional and nurturing component to the family.

As a helper to her husband, she carries a huge load of complementing his leadership in the home. One of the major responsibilities God has given her is to trust and submit to her husband's leadership. Nothing will help her children become obedient and respectful from their hearts as much as this character trait and the actions they observe in her.

The reason this is true is because her submission to her husband is her submission to God and the way He has delegated and ordered the principle of authority in human relationships. This joyful submission to God will be seen and internalized by her children. It will also help them learn their own submission to God through obedience to their parents and respect for authority in the broader relationships of their lives.

As a woman trusts and submits to her husband's leadership, she is set free to accomplish the other responsibilities God has given to her because her husband cannot lead her and their household without her support and help. Her trust in his leadership, more than anything else, is what gives him confidence to take on his daunting responsibility as husband and father. A husband has not been given a task by God to make his wife submit. Rather, he has been commanded by God to love her as Christ loved the Church and gave Himself up for her.

Likewise, her submission is based on her own free will to fulfill the crucial role God has assigned to her. When she is obedient to her Lord, she moves into the "sweet spot" of what it means to be her husband's helper. This enables both her and her husband to function in a godly and loving unity that will empower them to bring up their children "in the discipline and instruction of the Lord" (Ephesians 6:4b). This godly balance in their relationship will enable them to experience the unhindered and unlimited power of God to help them become the parents He wants them to be.

A third crucial aspect of a woman being a helper to her husband is the tremendous amount of responsibility she assumes in the running of the home. Paul refers to this responsibility in his pastoral training document sent to Titus. The apostle writes this concerning the responsibility of older women:

> Older women likewise are to be reverent in their
> behavior, not malicious gossips nor enslaved to
> much wine, teaching what is good, so that they
> may encourage the young women to love their
> husbands, to love their children, to be sensible,
> pure, workers at home, kind, being subject to
> their own husbands, so that the word of God will
> not be dishonored.
>
> —Titus 2:3-5

It's important to focus on the phrase "workers at home." In the Greek text, this phrase is one word meaning "homeworkers." It's only found this one time in the New Testament and refers to "caring for the house," according to *Thayer's*. This word, along with the other directives to a wife and mother, indicate that the highest calling on her life by God is be the "keeper of the home."

D. Edmond Hiebert, a biblical scholar in the middle of the 20th century, had this to say:

> The devoted wife and mother finds her absorbing interest in the innumerable duties of the home. These demand unsparing self-giving and may subject her to the temptation to be irritable and harsh in her demands on members of her household. She must therefore cultivate the virtue of being "kind," i.e. benevolent, heartily doing what is good and beneficial to others, especially those of her household.

One of the most powerful messages I've read regarding this high calling of wife and mother comes from Dorothy Kelley Patterson, a seminary-trained pastor's wife. In her essay, "The High Calling of Wife and Mother in Biblical Perspective," she reflected on her early days of marriage and motherhood as a professional woman with two young children.

"I can see in looking back that my first and freshest energies, not to mention the most productive part of my day, were devoted to professional pursuits away from home," she wrote. After moving with her husband into a pastoral church ministry, she confessed, "My theological training seemed a waste for the task of motherhood before me."

During the frustration of this time, she earnestly sought God's mind in His Word, the Bible, for direction in her life as a woman, a wife, and a mother. After her study, she made a commitment to the authority of God's Word, which led her to a point of surrender in her God-ordained identity and role. She then wrote this:

> Consequently, my chosen role of wife and mother took on new significance; my extensive academic preparation and professional experience I viewed in a new light; my commitment to marriage and home gained an added dimension—a divine contractual relationship reaching beyond my husband and me to include the Creator God Himself, who said, "Therefore what God has joined together, let man not separate."

Regarding our late 20th century culture and society, she added:

> Bearing a new liberated identity, many women have devoted themselves to ambitious busyness everywhere but in the home. They are enmeshed in overwhelming voluntarism to achieve accolades and recognition in the community, or they are surrogate wives and mothers dedicated to hatching professional pursuits that promise power and pocketbook. Women have been liberated right out of the genuine freedom they enjoyed for centuries to oversee the home, rear the children, and pursue personal creativity; they have been brainwashed to believe that the absence of a titled, payroll occupation enslaves a woman to failure, boredom, and imprisonment within the confines of home.

It is because of this terrible distortion promoted in our secular society—a distortion that's also infecting our churches—that we need to hear from God Himself who has spoken definitively in His eternal Word. Listen to His perspective from Proverbs 31:10-31:

An excellent wife, who can find?
For her worth is far above jewels.
The heart of her husband trusts in her,
And he will have no lack of gain.
She does him good and not evil
All the days of her life.
She looks for wool and flax
And works with her hands in delight.
She is like merchant ships;
She brings her food from afar.
She rises also while it is still night
And gives food to her household
And portions to her maidens.
She considers a field and buys it;
From her earnings she plants a vineyard.
She girds herself with strength
And makes her arms strong.
She senses that her gain is good;
Her lamp does not go out at night.
She stretches out her hands to the distaff;
And her hands grasp the spindle.
She extends her hand to the poor,
And she stretches out her hands to the needy.
She is not afraid of the snow for her household,
For all her household are clothed with scarlet.
She makes coverings for herself;
Her clothing is fine linen and purple.
Her husband is known in the gates,
When he sits among the elders of the land.
She makes linen garments and sells them,
And supplies belts to the tradesmen.
Strength and dignity are her clothing,
And she smiles at the future.

She opens her mouth in wisdom,
And the teaching of kindness is on her tongue.
She looks well to the ways of her household,
And does not eat the bread of idleness.
Her children rise up and bless her;
Her husband also, and he praises her, saying,
"Many daughters have done nobly,
But you excel them all."
Charm is deceitful and beauty is vain,
But a woman who fears the LORD, she shall be
praised.
Give her the product of her hands,
And let her works praise her in the gates.

I know a Proverbs 31 woman. She's my wife, Grace.

At the risk of being self-serving, I want to tell you a bit about Grace. We were married on July 10, 1954, in Pasadena, California. She was just nineteen and I was twenty-two. We had spent the majority of our year-and-a-half courting days serving together in a little Baptist church. I directed the choir while she played the piano and organ.

We also worked with the junior high and high school students. While I considered her the most beautiful girl at the Christian college we attended, one of the main reasons I married her was because of the character quality of self-sacrifice she exhibited. She never complained that we spent too much time ministering to the young people or doing what we did to maintain the quality of our church's musical worship.

Less than two years after we were married, I became the solo pastor of a small neighborhood church in Alhambra, California, while still carrying twelve units in seminary. With everything going on in the early years of our marriage, she gave birth to four wonderful children by the time she was twenty-five.

She taught piano to supplement our small income and folded diapers for a period of eight years. (No Pampers in those days!) She shopped for food, usually with our four young ones on tricycles, scooters, and in a wagon two or three times a week. She washed our clothes with an old-fashioned washer with a roller wringer and hung them out to dry on a clothesline in the back yard. She ironed much of those clothes. She cleaned our house with not enough help from me. She sewed matching clothes for our kids that drew raves from the ladies of the church. She directed the children's Sunday school and played the piano or organ for our worship service.

Since I would come to church on Sunday mornings around 7 a.m. to get everything ready, she would dress all four kids and have them at Sunday school on time, looking like they had stepped out of a photo shoot. I helped her bathe the kids Saturday night, but she didn't get much else from me.

I preached Sunday mornings and Sunday nights as well as a devotional at our Wednesday night prayer services. I led our youth ministry, the musical worship, and took the offering. Sometimes I played the trumpet and directed the choir at Christmas and Easter.

With her tremendous help, I led our Vacation Bible School and trips to a Navajo reservation with a team of adults and youth. I did all the church visitation and conducted the funerals and weddings. In addition, I was still in seminary and taking twelve units of graduate study. And I painted two days a week for a while and then replaced that side income by working in commercial real estate.

Grace's help in my pastoral ministry has continued for more than sixty years. Her presence and amazing support of God's work through my life has been absolutely and immeasurably significant and necessary. I cannot begin to imagine where I'd be today without her.

In addition to being such a help and support to me, Grace has had an amazingly effective ministry to women and children throughout the years. This has been on top of her gifted ability to play the piano. At every church we've served in, she provided excellent piano and organ accompaniment without pay. God honored her by enabling her to make a CD of hymns and gospel songs—played by her hands on the piano—that has been used by God to bless hundreds of people. One of the great joys of my life has been hearing her soul-reaching music all our lives together.

One other area I must mention concerning Grace's fulfillment of her God-given role has to do with her contentment with our financial status and our living conditions. She has always been willing to live creatively within the income God has provided us. Money has never been a source of tension in our family, even during the first ten years of our lives together when were so poor we didn't bother to open a bank account.

We have lived in eight homes in more than sixty years of marriage. In the first few years of marriage, when two of our four children were born, we lived in a rickety old church parsonage that doubled as classrooms and the kitchen for the church. I received no complaints from her.

In each move, she saw God's hand in what we were doing and joyfully embraced our lives as God's will for us. This included a time recently when we sold our only home and moved into a two-bedroom apartment. We did that because God made it clear that we needed the equity in our home to take care of us when we no longer could do that ourselves. That process of downsizing and discarding a lot of the "stuff" that we had acquired over the years was accepted by her with the same trust in God she had displayed in every other move.

I share this because I want you to know that God's wise and loving appointment of women as wives and mothers is an incomparable contribution to the thriving health of every family, including ours. What God has revealed about the woman's role in the home and society is not theory; it's divine revelation and a powerful reality.

Besides the high calling of being a wife and mother, there's crucial contribution that a woman brings to parenting and family life, which is explained in Titus 2:3-5 and bears repeating:

> Older women likewise are to be reverent in their behavior, not malicious gossips nor enslaved to much wine, teaching what is good, so that they may encourage the young women to love their husbands, to love their children, to be sensible, pure, workers at home, kind, being subject to their own husbands, so that the word of God will not be dishonored.

This passage is a helpful combination of godliness, submission, and spiritual focus for a woman in her role within the family, but the part I want to highlight is the encouragement for women to love their husbands and love their children. The words used in the Greek are *philandrous*, which means "lovers of husbands," and *philoteknous*, which means "child-lovers."

These are compound words uniting *phileo* with the words for husband and children. The word used for husbands to love their wives in Ephesians 5 is *agapao*. While these words are used interchangeably several times in the New Testament, it's evident to many biblical scholars that there is a distinction between them.

Thayer's indicates this: "As to the distinction between *agapao* and *phileo*, the former . . . properly denotes a love founded in admiration, veneration, esteem . . . but *phileo* denotes an inclination prompted by sense and emotion. Christ bids us to *agapao* (not *phileo*) our enemies in Matthew 5:44 because love as an emotion cannot be commanded, but only love as a choice."

Johannes Louw and Eugene Nida, in their *Greek-English*

Lexicon of the New Testament, refer to *phileo* as having "love or affection for someone or something based on association." In referring to *agapao,* they write that it is "generally assumed to mean moral goodwill that proceeds from esteem, principle, or duty rather than attraction of charm."

The passage in Titus uses *phileo* love to describe the love between a mother and her children. While *phileo* and *agapao* have distinction, the scholarship is not compelling to see *phileo* love as inferior to *agapao* love, as some biblical scholars assert.

To me, this is made clear in John 16:27 when Jesus is speaking to His disciples and says, "For the Father Himself loves [*phileo*] you, because you have loved [*phileo*] Me and have believed that I came forth from the Father."

This is a use of the word explaining that we who follow Jesus are now associated with Him and the Father in a supernatural and intimate relationship. We belong to them. We have become "their own" and they have become "our own."

This emphasis on association ties in beautifully to a woman's relationship to her husband and her children. Her love for them is divinely focused on the connection God has built into her heart and mind that is natural and powerful. When she gives her heart and mind and body to her husband, she is entrusting herself to his protection, care, and leadership.

This is such an amazing act of faith on her part that God calls a man's infidelity to that relationship treachery in Malachi 2:14-16. When a woman conceives and bears a child, a relationship of love and belonging is established that's astounding in its depth and intensity. This special love for her husband and children that God reveals in Titus 2:4 is made more powerful because of this God-given connection and sense of belonging in these two relationships. All of this is inherent in this indispensable word for love—*phileo.*

The responsibility of a woman to love (*phileo*) her husband

and her children is not expressed by a command. This kind of emotional love is *built* into a woman by God. She naturally has affection, but it must also be developed and trained. This is the word Paul uses in instructing older women to "encourage" the younger women to love their husbands and their children.

Women have been given a wonderful gift of nurturing and emotion that's essential in the lives of their husbands and children. This gift needs to be used in a way that God intended, which requires self-control, discipline, wisdom, and a strong sense of duty before Him. This gift is strongly present in every woman but can be focused in many directions.

Too many times, this gift is focused on people and ministries outside the home. I can't help but think of some women I've known who've had great compassion for abandoned children and at-risk teenagers. When they got involved with social programs to help these kids, I saw how their children and families were neglected—there are just only so many hours in a day and only so much energy in a body.

This passage in Titus 2:3-5 is a powerful corrective to those who go down that road. Raising children, as nearly every parent will agree, is paramount in importance and is the topic of my next chapter.

GODLY AUTHORITY AS IT APPLIES TO THE GODLINESS OF CHILDREN

One more important truth needs to be emphasized about the end goal of parenting, and it's this: a child's obedience leads to godliness. Ephesians 6:1-4 sums up God's direction succinctly:

> Children, obey your parents in the Lord, for this is right. HONOR YOUR FATHER AND MOTHER (which is the first commandment with a promise), SO THAT IT MAY BE WELL WITH YOU, AND THAT YOU MAY LIVE LONG ON EARTH. Fathers, do not provoke your children to anger, but bring them up in the discipline and instruction of the Lord.

The Importance of Principles of Obedience

I find it difficult to overestimate the importance of children being obedient to God's authority through their obedience to their parents. This is a major concern of God's, which can be seen throughout His communication to us in the Scriptures. Here's another key form of communication from Proverbs 6:20-23:

> My son, observe the commandment of your father
> And do not forsake the teaching of your mother;
> Bind them continually on your heart;
> Tie them around your neck.
> When you walk about, they will guide you;
> When you sleep, they will watch over you;

And when you awake, they will talk to you.
For the commandment is a lamp and the teaching
is light;
And reproofs for discipline are the way of life.

The result of the lack of parental training and discipline is graphically laid out in Proverbs 23:13-14:

Do not hold back discipline from the child,
Although you strike him with the rod, he will
not die.
You shall strike him with the rod
And rescue his soul from Sheol.

The urgency of parental discipline is manifested in Proverbs 19:18:

Discipline your son while there is hope,
And do not desire his death.

The same vein of thought continues in Proverbs 13:24:

He who withholds his rod hates his son,
But he who loves him disciplines him diligently.

My advice in this chapter is based on many years of raising our four children and counseling scores of other parents in the discipline of their children, as well as the wise experience of many other authors and counselors regarding the issue of obedience from the heart and the will of the child.

I'll start with the literal reading of the Hebrew phrase in Proverbs 13:24, quoted above, which is this: "seeks him diligently with discipline." Bringing that phrase into this crucial principle admonishes you to not just seek obedience in outward behavior but to also seek it from the heart and will of the child. Another way of saying this is to look for a willful spirit and attitude.

Do not be content with only outward behavior. Take the time to help your children surrender their wills to the Lord and to you as their parents.

The author of Hebrews makes it clear that this issue of discipline for obedience is about "striving against sin" (Hebrews 12:4b). Since evil is a terrible reality that seeks to destroy us, people who recoil from this strong emphasis on discipline minimize that evil and fantasize that their children are basically good. This flies directly in the face of God's clear teaching in Psalm 51:5 in which David declares, "Behold, I was brought forth in iniquity, and in sin my mother conceived me."

This concept of "original sin" is also indicated in Romans 5:12:

> Therefore, just as through one man sin entered
> into the world, and death through sin, and so
> death spread to all men, because all sinned.

Paul explains further in Romans 5:18b,19b that "through one transgression there resulted condemnation to all men . . . through the one man's disobedience the many were made sinners."

I like how Wayne Grudem, in *Systematic Theology*, terms original sin as "inherited sin," explaining, "I have used the phrase 'inherited sin' rather than the more common designation 'original sin' because the phrase 'original sin' seems so easily to be misunderstood to refer to Adam's first sin, rather than to the sin that is ours as a result of Adam's fall." The reason this truth is so important is that it can inform your view of humanity, your anthropology. And your view of humanity determines how you bring about godly and righteous lives in your children as well as yourself.

There is an opposing train of thought that believes humans are basically good. Therefore, the best way to train your children is to praise the positive and ignore the negative. If you'll just keep them happy and their lives pleasant, they will automatically do what is right and thrive. This becomes a child-raising philosophy, however, that is permissive, indulgent, and enabling in unrighteous behavior.

As I've described, Grace and I raised four children and have supported them in their raising of sixteen grandchildren. We have consistently noticed in all of the grandchildren, as well as in our four offspring, the manifestation of fallen Adam, beginning at a very young age! This was always connected to them not getting their own way in the time they thought appropriate. Children need, and in fact desire, your help to learn obedience and live in God's righteous and loving ways.

This crucial truth does not support the notion that God's way in Scripture is mean-spirited, oppressive, or abusive. This biblical concept of discipline is clearly connected to love and is God's way of doing what is best for your child in God's eyes and for the child's highest good. This connection of discipline and love is beautifully expressed in Hebrews 12:5-7:

> And you have forgotten the exhortation which is
> addressed to you as sons,
> "MY SON, DO NOT REGARD LIGHTLY THE DISCIPLINE
> OF THE LORD,
> NOR FAINT WHEN YOU ARE REPROVED BY HIM;
> FOR THOSE WHOM THE LORD LOVES HE DISCIPLINES,
> AND HE SCOURGES EVERY SON WHOM HE RECEIVES."
> It is for discipline that you endure; God deals with
> you as with sons, for what son is there whom his
> father does not discipline?

The writer of Hebrews then follows up with honest and encouraging words in verse 11:

> All discipline for the moment seems not to be
> joyful, but sorrowful; yet to those who have been

trained by it, afterwards it yields the peaceful fruit of righteousness.

That's what I would call the sweet spot of parental discipline.

Loving Instruction and Discipline

This leads me to relate several more crucial principles in the parent's lovingly training their children in God's ways.

In Ephesians 6:4, Paul reminds fathers, since they bear the primary load of leading the family and disciplining the children, that they are not to "provoke" their children to anger but bring them up in the discipline and instruction of the Lord.

This is an incredibly important concept since many children have learned to hate authority because of the way that authority provoked them to anger. Paul writes in a similar way in Colossians 3:21 where he coaches, "Fathers, do not exasperate your children, so that they will not lose heart."

The word Paul uses in Ephesians is *parorgidzo*, which means "to rouse to wrath, to provoke, exasperate, anger," according to *Thayer's*. The verb is the present, active imperative, which means it's a command that is continuous and therefore needs to be always in operation. The word he uses in the Colossians letter is *erethidzo*, which means "to stir up, excite, stimulate." Erethidzo can be used either positively or negatively, but when used in a negative context, it simply means "to provoke." The negative context of Colossians is evident because of the consequence of this provocation—"that they may not lose heart."

These injunctions given to fathers may seem brief and small, but they are crucial. Nothing is sadder than to come across children who have "lost heart." It's been often said that our discipline should aim at breaking their will, but not their spirit.

The breaking of their will helps them surrender to the authority God has placed in their lives. In fact, this is a primary component of being a disciple, a follower of Jesus, who said in Mark 8:34b-35:

> "If anyone wishes to come after Me, he must deny himself, and take up his cross and follow Me. For whoever wishes to save his life will lose it, but whoever loses his life for My sake and the gospel's will save it."

Helping children submit to God's authority in their lives by training them to obey their parents is preparing them to receive Jesus as their Savior and Lord. This is the ultimate goal of parenting. This is what Paul meant when he said you are to bring up your children in the nurture and admonition of the Lord. David Martyn Lloyd-Jones, one of the greatest expository preachers of the 20th century, writes:

> In the forefront of the minds of Christian parents must ever be the thought that the children are to be brought up in the knowledge of the Lord Jesus Christ as Savior and as Lord. That is the peculiar task to which Christian parents alone are called. This is not only their supreme task: their greatest desire and ambition for their children should be that they should come to know the Lord Jesus Christ as their Savior and as their Lord.

When that is done in a godly and loving way, their hearts and spirits will soar and thrive because they have lost their lives for Jesus' sake. Witnessing the life of a well-trained child is such a privilege, and that's because of the power of submission. When God-appointed authority is implemented in God's way, the result is great freedom and health.

There are also three important words Paul uses in Ephesians

to consider. The first, normally translated "to bring them up," is *ektrepho*, which also means "to nourish up to maturity, to nourish, to nurture, to bring up," according to *Thayer's*. This has to do with providing the means to sustain life and promote growth. It can have the connotation of support in a general way, and it includes the thought of education.

One of the synonyms *ektrepho* is connected to is our word *cherish*. This refers to holding or treating something or someone dearly. The emphasis of nurture includes "mental and spiritual training with love and tenderness" (*Funk & Wagnalls Standard Dictionary*).

The second word Paul uses is *paideia*. This comprehensive word can be used as "the whole training and education of children," according to *Thayer's*. It can also refer to "instruction which aims at virtue" including chastisement. Then the word *chastening*, which refers to corporal punishment with a "rod or whip" (*Funk & Wagnalls*), is "wholly corrective and merciful in intent and result." The third word Paul uses is translated as "instruction" from the Greek word *nouthesia*, which means "admonition, exhortation" and has the connotation of correction and urging someone toward righteous choices and behavior. All of this discussion promotes a goal of loving and caring instruction and training that engages children's hearts and does not squelch their spirit, producing the peaceful fruit of righteousness.

Parental Guidelines for Loving Discipline

Let me identify some ways that we, as parents, provoke, anger, and exasperate our children. While I'm certain many experts on child-raising have addressed this issue better than I can, I'm going to make some observations from my own experience as a father and pastor for over sixty years. Many of these observations take into account my failures as a parent and those of other parents. Here are some ideas to keep in mind:

1. **Don't overcorrect your kids.** If you try to correct too many behaviors, you will overwhelm and discourage your children. Ask God's Spirit to help you discern what are the most important issues your children are dealing with, given their age.

   It's important that you distinguish between what are childish mistakes, e.g. spilling milk, and what is pure disobedience, like going out in the street despite constant reminders not to do that. You can be greatly helped in this process by looking for the positive traits and aspects your children do that reveal an obedient heart. Praise and encourage them in that behavior.

   In the early years of my pastoral ministry, I was having lunch with one of our elders. While we were talking about how things were going in his life and with his family, he told me he was quite concerned about his wife's discipline of their young daughter. "She spends most of her time correcting our girl and nitpicking her to death," he said.

   This man was an elementary school educator, so he knew a lot about working with children. He said that he had talked to his wife about "lightening up," but she wouldn't change the way she parented the child.

   This dear girl began a downward spiral that eventually ended up with her reaching her teen years and running away and living on the streets. I don't know how much impact this mother's overcorrection had in this sad outcome, but it's likely a considerable amount.

   John Bunyan, the 16th century Puritan preacher

who wrote *Pilgrim's Progress*, advised parents, "Let those words you speak to them in your reproof be both sober, *few*, and pertinent" (italics mine).

2. **Be on the lookout for a lack of consistency in training a child.** If you're strong in correcting wrong behavior on Monday but ignore that same misbehavior on Thursday, then your actions bring confusion and frustration to a child. A lack of consistency is high on the list because of its prevalence among parents. You can sometimes "wear down" in the responsibility of training your children, or your emotions are too much in control, or you're just lazy.

3. **Be alert to injustice.** Another place of parental failure occurs when you discipline them for a behavior that you're not absolutely certain happened. This injustice is highly damaging to the heart and trust of a child.

4. **Favoring one child over another.** One of the most devastating ways you can exasperate your children and cause them to lose heart is when you favor one child over another. It's difficult to cite a more ungodly action or attitude on display. The potential for stimulating and promoting evil in the lives of your children is at its highest when you play favorites because there is such power to demean and destroy in showing partiality. Sadly, favoritism is present in far too many families.

5. **Going off the deep end of punishment.** Another failure is that of punishing too harshly for the "crime" committed. Children have a natural sense of justice. When that is violated, the result is discouragement and anger.

6. **Disciplining in anger, either verbally or corporally, is highly common and highly damaging.** This is where children learn that when you are bigger, stronger, and older, you have the right to be violent. I will never forget when one of our sons, in his preteen years, was verbally disrespectful to his mother. I quickly slapped him across his face. I was immediately convicted that I had done physically to him what he had verbally done to his mother. I quickly acknowledged my anger and confessed my wrong to my son.

7. **Give serious attention to your modeling submission to God.** Failure to lead by example creates a discouragement to obedience that can last a lifetime. Not placing yourself as a parent under the authority and ways of God seriously weakens any hope that your children will take your words of correction and reproof seriously. God spoke solemnly and powerfully to His people, recorded in Deuteronomy 6:5-7, in this manner:

> You shall love the LORD your God with all your heart and with all your soul and with all your might. These words, which I am commanding you today, shall be on your heart. You shall teach them diligently to your sons and shall talk of them when you sit in your house and when you walk by the way and when you lie down and when you rise up.

This exhortation from our Heavenly Father unequivocally indicates that any instruction, correction, and training of your children should be dependent on the reality of your commitment to God's Word and God's ways. If that is present, then your children will have a genuine opportunity to listen and follow in God's ways. If it's not present, they will begin their process of hearing and obeying God with a huge deficit. This limitation can certainly be overcome by God's sovereign grace, but every parent will be held accountable for the "stumbling block" we put in the way of our children.

8. **Teach them what's behind the way you're parenting them.** You need to avoid conveying to your children that your motive for disciplining them stems from the inconvenience, annoyance, and disruption their disobedience causes you.

John Bunyan again has some pearls of wisdom to share: "Let all of this be mixed with such love, pity, and compassion of spirit that, if possible, they may be convinced you dislike not their persons, but their sins. This is God's way." Referring to when and how corporal punishment should be employed in our training of our children, he thoughtfully counsels in the language of his time—the late 1500s:

> See if fair words will win them from evil. This is God's way with His children.
>
> If you are driven to the rod, then strike advisedly in cool blood and soberly show them: (a) their fault; (b) how much it is against your heart to deal with them in this way; (c) that what you do you do in conscience to God and love to their souls; and (d) tell them that if fair means would have done, none of this severity should have been.

This, I have proved it, will be a means to afflict their hearts as well as their bodies, and it being the way that God deals with His, it is the most likely to accomplish its end . . . follow all this with prayer to God for them, and leave the issue to Him. "Foolishness is bound in the heart of a child; but the rod of correction shall drive it far from him" (Proverbs 22:15).

All discipline at all levels must be done with the love of the child at the heart of the process. When this is true, God's Spirit will support you in avoiding these many ways we fail our children in training them to be obedient to God and to us from their hearts. He will also support you in conveying to your children that you love them and only desire God's best for them.

Understanding these principles of God's authority in the family will prepares you for learning how His authority is to be expressed in the Church, which is the main message of the rest of my book.

GODLY AUTHORITY AS IT APPLIES TO THE CHURCH

There's no place on Earth where clarity concerning spiritual, godly authority is more important than in the Church of which Jesus is the Head. It's in this sphere where division among God's people is most on display. And it's also in this sphere where unity is most crucial to the validation of the gospel message.

In His high-priestly prayer for the Church in John 17:20-21, Jesus spoke to His Father with these words:

> I do not ask on behalf of these alone [the apostles], but for those also who believe in Me through their word; that they may all be one; even as You, Father, are in Me and I in You, that they also may be in Us, so that the world may believe that You sent Me.

Unity can only be achieved when there is clarity about authority and submission to that God-ordained authority. As in every other sphere of human existence, clarity about authority begins with God, a topic that I dealt with extensively in chapter 3 when I made the following crystal-clear assertion: God the Father is the only final source of authority.

With that statement as our foundation, His authority is delegated to God the Son in key areas of the divine administration, including the Church, and then God the Spirit "proceeds from" and is sent by both the Father and the Son. All of the members of the Godhead are equal in essence, substance, value, and importance. In the issue of authority, Father, Son, and Holy Spirit each have distinct roles and are part of a function and order that is governed by the Father.

God's Authority Delegated to Jesus

I start by reminding you from Ephesians 1:20b-22 that God the Father, after raising Jesus the Son from the dead:

> . . . seated Him at His right hand in the heavenly places, far above all rule and authority and power and dominion, and every name that is named, not only in this age but also in the one to come. And He put all things in subjection under His feet, and gave Him as *head over all things to the church* (with italics added for emphasis).

As far as God the Father is concerned, Jesus Christ, the Son of God, is already in a place of exaltation and authority over "all rule and authority and power and dominion, and every name that is named." Most authorities on earth, it can be said with a great degree of confidence, do not know this amazing truth. But we in the Church of Jesus Christ are glad to bow before Him as the only head of the Church.

Jesus Christ affirmed His position as head of the Church in Matthew 28:18-20:

> And Jesus came up and spoke to them, saying, "All authority has been given to Me in Heaven and on earth. Go therefore and make disciples of all the nations, baptizing them in the name of the Father and the Son and the Holy Spirit, teaching them to observe all that I commanded you; and lo, I am with you always, even to the end of the age."

In this passage, Jesus not only affirmed the authority the Father had delegated to Him, but He clearly delegated His authority to the apostles. This delegation of authority has become widely known as "the Great Commission." This same commission is given in John 20:21b-22, where He says:

> "Peace be with you; as the Father has sent Me,
> I also send you." And when He had said this, He
> breathed on them and said to them, "Receive the
> Holy Spirit."

Another noteworthy Scripture is Luke 24:45-49, where Luke records several important details about Christ's commission to the apostles:

> Then He opened their minds to understand
> the Scriptures, and He said to them, "Thus it
> is written, that the Christ would suffer and
> rise again from the dead the third day, and
> that repentance for forgiveness of sins would
> be proclaimed in His name to all the nations,
> beginning from Jerusalem. You are witnesses of
> these things. And behold, I am sending forth the
> promise of My Father upon you; but you are to
> stay in the city until you are clothed with power
> from on high."

Finally, this commission is recorded in Acts 1:4-8:

> Gathering them together, He commanded them
> not to leave Jerusalem, but to wait for what the
> Father had promised, "Which," He said, "you
> heard of from Me; for John baptized with water,
> but you will be baptized with the Holy Spirit not
> many days from now."

So when they had come together, they were asking Him, saying, "Lord, is it at this time You are restoring the kingdom to Israel?" He said to them, "It is not for you to know times or epochs which the Father has fixed by His own authority; but you will receive power when the Holy Spirit has come upon you; and you shall be My witnesses both in Jerusalem, and in all Judea and Samaria, and even to the remotest part of the earth."

In each of these four passages, two important truths were established:

1. Jesus is the Head of the Church and has complete authority over it.

2. He clearly delegated His authority to the eleven disciples, called apostles in Acts, to lead the Church in the proclamation of the gospel to the ends of the earth.

Except for Matthew's account, these recordings indicate a crucial truth that was emphasized by Jesus: the apostles were not to try to fulfill their commission on their own. Instead, they were to wait until they were given the Holy Spirit of promise from the Father so they would have His power to accomplish all that He intended for them and through them.

Many books have been written and many sermons have been preached about the content and implementation of the Great Commission, and I've preached a few of those homilies myself because Christ's words are rich in meaning and powerful in strategy for the ministry of the Church on earth. What's clear is that we can learn a great deal from how Jesus delegated authority to the apostles.

Jesus' Authority Delegated to the Apostles

How were the apostles prepared to receive Jesus' authority and commission?

The first thing I want to point out is that Jesus spent most of His time in His earthly ministry with these men. While it's true that He also devoted a significant amount of time with the multitudes in many venues and settings, His priority was clearly the training and preparation of twelve men to be the foundation and leaders of His Church. Few have considered this priority more than Robert E. Coleman in his classic, insightful book, *The Master Plan of Evangelism*:

> It all started by Jesus calling a few men to follow Him. This revealed immediately the direction His evangelistic strategy would take. His concern was not with programs to reach the multitudes, but with men whom the multitudes would follow. Remarkable as it may seem, Jesus started to gather these men before He ever organized an evangelistic campaign or even preached a sermon in public. Men were to be His method of winning the world to God.

Coleman goes on to explain that this emphasis on the few was deliberate because "the more concentrated the size of the group being taught, the greater the opportunity for effective instruction." He underlined his point even more when he wrote, "Jesus devoted most of His remaining life on earth to these few disciples. He literally staked His whole ministry upon them." Coleman's book does a great job explaining what Jesus' preparation of the apostles looked like in content, strategy, and process. By the time Jesus ascended into heaven, they were well prepared by their

Master, the Son of Man and the Son of God.

I am fully aware that this emphasis on the apostles could be interpreted as neglecting the important place women have in the building of the Church. What I'm saying is that the issue at hand is the position of authority in the Church. My point is that the place of human authority in Scripture is assigned to men, and this clearly includes the sphere of the Church.

As for women, they have an important role and assignment in God's plan as well, as I will describe in greater detail in Chapter 16.

A second part of the apostles' training included dealing with their failure and imperfection. This is most notably apparent in Peter's passionate denial of Jesus, which took place in the courtyard of the high priest while He, Jesus, was being interrogated by "the high priest; and all the chief priests and the elders and the scribes gathered together" (Mark 14:53b).

That this was no small aberration or a slip of the tongue on the part of Peter is indicated by the fact that he denied knowing Jesus three times, the last with cursing and swearing. In addition, this failure to tell the truth impacted Peter deeply in his heart because "he began to weep" following the crowing of the rooster a second time (14:72b).

The other apostles, except perhaps John, weren't present but they also denied the Lord when they left Him and fled the garden where He was accosted and taken by a mob sent by the "chief priests and the elders and the scribes." Even though Jesus knew this denial and abandonment was going to take place, it must have grieved Him deeply that these men in whom He had invested so much time, love, and training had failed Him miserably.

No one felt any worse than Peter. After all, it was Peter who boasted that "even though all may fall away, yet I will not" in Mark 14:29b. After hearing that, Jesus explained to Peter:

"Truly I say to you, that this very night, before a rooster crows twice, you yourself will deny Me three times" But Peter kept saying insistently, "Even if I have to die with You, I will not deny You!"

—Mark 14:30b-31a

Jesus, who knows the past, present, and future, knew that wasn't true. One of the most amazing truths about Jesus is how well and intimately He knows us, His servants. He is truly the High Priest who can "sympathize with our weaknesses" (Hebrews 4:15b).

Following His death on the Cross, the rest of this story unfolds as an encouraging drama, beginning at explaining how a scene at the Sea of Galilee became another crucial manifestation of the risen Lord to His disciples (John 21:1-17). The reason this happened at the Sea of Galilee was because Peter and six other disciples had decided to go fishing.

What happened next followed other appearances of the risen Lord Jesus to these men. The fact that Jesus was alive had to be very wonderful for these men but also very convicting. It would be one thing to deny and abandon their beloved leader if He had not risen from the dead. Peter must have just been unaware of how powerful the forces of darkness were and how much he misjudged his own power and person.

But Jesus had risen and conquered death, just as He said He would. Now the weight of the disciples' denial had grown exponentially, especially for Peter, who had denied that the Son of God was everything He said He was and everything they had come to believe He was. The guilt and sense of failure was so heavy on Peter and the others that they decided to go back to what they knew best—fishing. John, who was present in this event, tells us dejectedly that they fished all night and caught nothing. It would be hard to describe the sense of failure and depression that these men were experiencing in this setting.

Precisely as the time of this devastating failure, Jesus appeared on the shore. His acceptance and grace towards them was powerfully made known by His presence, a fire to warm them, breakfast to feed them, and, amazingly, helping them to catch an overload of fish before they came to shore. This acceptance by Jesus in the midst of their failure was crucial to them being able to fulfill His commission to them. They were flawed and broken human beings; they knew it and Jesus knew it. Their only hope was His grace, which they experienced deeply.

That grace was not permissive, however, because Jesus confronted them, through Peter, with their failure and began the painful, healing, and restorative process after breakfast. This happened when Jesus asked Peter three times if he loved Him.

The first time Jesus asked him, He wanted to know if Peter still thought his love for Jesus was greater than any of the others. This is what Peter had boasted in the presence of his fellow apostles. Now he had to admit in their presence that his love for Jesus was not better than theirs and was not even of the highest kind of *agape* love.

The best he could confess was a type of love that was "fond, human, emotional affection" for Jesus, according to *Thayer's*. This Jesus fully accepted when, in His third time of questioning Peter, He used this level of love with the word Peter had been using, which was *phileo*. While this word is not a weak word for love, it is, as I've noted, a love based more on sense and emotion and association, indicating a meaningful friendship. Jesus was not condemning Peter here. He was merely confronting him with his weakness and limitation in his own strength.

Following each of Jesus' three questions, He responded to Peter, and to the others by implication, with a renewed commission and a declared trust in spite of his and their failure. Those words of renewed trust were, "Tend My lambs . . . Shepherd My sheep . . . Tend My sheep" (21:15b, 16b, 17b).

A very important truth is revealed here about Jesus' expectations of His servant/leaders. He does not demand perfection, but He does demand honesty. Jesus can always work with and through us if we walk in honesty. This is what John was referring to in 1 John 1:7:

> But if we walk in the Light as He Himself is in
> the Light, we have fellowship with one another,
> and the blood of Jesus His Son cleanses us from
> all sin.

God is always working in and through flawed human beings. He is near to those who are "humble and contrite of spirit" (Isaiah 66:2b). For any person in leadership, an indispensable qualification is the honesty and humility that confesses human weakness and sinfulness. Those seeking and receiving forgiveness and cleansing are leaders that God can trust with authority, and this included the apostles.

A third area of preparation for the apostles was that of united prayer. The importance of prayer in doing the Father's will was modeled for the apostles by Jesus Himself, who frequently took time to be in fellowship with the Father and be dependent upon the Father in prayer, especially during times of intense activity. Luke 5:16 tells us, "But Jesus Himself would often slip away to the wilderness and pray."

The need for united prayer was also modeled by Jesus in the garden of Gethsemane. In Matthew's account, He took Peter, James, and John with Him into a secluded area. There He confessed to them, "My soul is deeply grieved, to the point of death; remain here and keep watch with Me" (Matthew 26:38b).

After He prayed for an hour, He came back and found the three men sleeping. This was repeated twice more, and each time they were still sleeping. His question betrayed His disappointment: "So, you men could not keep watch with me for one hour?" (26:40b).

You could say that the sequence of Peter's boast that he would never deny Jesus, sleeping in the garden during the time of Jesus' agonized prayer, and denying Him in the courtyard of the High Priest is extremely telling about the importance of prayer! Perhaps his failure in this instance prepared him to eagerly obey Jesus' direction before His ascension in the first chapter of Acts.

Jesus made it clear that they were not to enter into the ministry of the Great Commission until they understood God's plan and received God's power through His Spirit. Their process of waiting is described in Acts 1:12-14. The eleven apostles were part of a gathering in the upper room where they were staying among "about one hundred and twenty persons" (1:15b). Their activity is described in verse 14a: "These all with one mind were continually devoting themselves to prayer."

As a result of God's people being led by the apostles and united with them in prayer, they were "all filled with the Holy Spirit" (Acts 2:4b). The connection between waiting on God in prayer and the filling and power of the Holy Spirit is inescapable. Prayer was not putting them in charge but getting them ready for what the Father was going to do through His Spirit in their lives.

The essence of prayer is dependence on and submission to God. This is the way He stoops to our weakness and limitation as flawed humans and accomplishes in and through us more than we could ever imagine or think.

You may rightly ask if this really works. Peter, sleeping instead of praying, was easy prey for the Enemy and his own human frailty in denying Jesus, yet the same man in prayer, which resulted in the filling of the Holy Spirit, powerfully confronted the entire Jewish leadership and nation with the truth about Jesus' life, death, and resurrection. The summary of his Pentecostal sermon was spoken with devastating conviction in Acts 2:36:

"Therefore let all the house of Israel know for certain that God has made Him both Lord and Christ—this Jesus whom you crucified."

The conviction of the Holy Spirit through Peter resulted in three thousand souls repenting, being baptized, and receiving the "gift of the Holy Spirit." Prayer became, through the leadership of the apostles, the dynamic and direction of the early Church. Jesus had prepared them well for their authority and ministry as apostles.

* * *

A fourth area of preparation for the apostles was the Holy Spirit's leading to replace Judas, who had betrayed the Lord. The purpose of this action is indicated by Peter in Acts 1:21-22:

"Therefore it is necessary that of the men who have accompanied us all the time that the Lord Jesus went in and out among us—beginning with the baptism of John until the day that He was taken up from us—one of these must become a witness with us of His resurrection."

They then put forward two men who met this qualification, Joseph and Mathias. The seriousness of this process is indicated by their prayer in Acts 1:24b-25:

"You, Lord, who know the hearts of all men, show which one of these two You have chosen to occupy this ministry and apostleship from which Judas turned aside to go to his own place."

Peter realized, by the leading of God's Spirit, that ministering as a team was God's way. The completion of the team of apostles was building on Jesus' original selection of the men who were to lead in completing His work on this earth. The principle here is crucial: The Triune God exists and functions as a team.

This was highlighted at the baptism of Jesus when the Spirit descended as a dove from heaven, and the voice of the Father uttered the words, "This is My beloved Son, in whom I am well-pleased" (Matthew 3:17b). The team had gathered to begin the crucial phase of redemption through the work of Jesus, the Son in becoming "the Lamb of God who takes away the sin of the world" (John 1:29b).

This concept of the team was ignored by Peter, however, when he boasted that all the other disciples might deny and forsake the Lord, but he would not. After Jesus' death, though, he made a turnaround in his thinking when, in Acts 2:14b under the power of God's Spirit, he "[took] his stand *with the eleven*" (with italics added for emphasis).

The plurality of leadership among the apostles is foundational for the plurality of elders in the church, which flows from the very nature and function of the Triune God, who has always existed in community as a family and as a team. This is why the completion of the apostolic team is important as revealed in Acts 1.

The fifth and final component of the apostles' preparation was that of divine power. Here is a quick summary: Jesus' words to His apostles were that they were not to leave Jerusalem and begin their ministry, but to:

> . . . wait for what the Father had promised,
> "Which," He said, "you heard of from Me; for John
> baptized with water, but you will be baptized with
> the Holy Spirit not many days from now."
>
> —Acts 1:4b-5

A few verses later, He declared, "you will receive power when the Holy Spirit has come upon you; and you shall be My witnesses both in Jerusalem, and in all Judea and Samaria, and even to the remotest part of the earth" (Acts 1:8).

This is where Jesus gave them the Father's plan and the Father's power to carry it out. The work they were to accomplish was a supernatural work and could only be accomplished with supernatural power infused into them by the indwelling Holy Spirit sent to them by both the Father and the Son (Acts 2:33).

The Holy Spirit Delegated to Guide the Apostles

When Jesus ascended into the heavens and returned to the Father, He expressed confidence and trust in these apostles to fulfill the commission He had given them. Their authority included at least three areas:

- teaching

- signs and wonders

- spiritual oversight of the Church

Regarding these three areas, there are two critical passages of Scripture where Jesus established the authority of the apostles in teaching God's Word for His people. The first is found in John 14:25-26:

> "These things I have spoken to you while abiding with you. But the Helper, the Holy Spirit, whom the Father will send in My name, He will teach you all things, and bring to your remembrance all that I said to you."

This was Jesus' promise to His apostles: that the Holy Spirit was going to complete Jesus' authoritative teaching and it would be based on remembering "all that I said to you."

Another passage of Scripture where Jesus conferred His authority on the apostles to establish God's words for His Church is found in John 16:12-14:

> "I have many more things to say to you, but you cannot bear them now. But when He, the Spirit of truth, comes, He will guide you into all the truth; for He will not speak on His own initiative, but whatever He hears, He will speak; and He will disclose to you what is to come. He will glorify Me, for He will take of Mine and will disclose it to you."

It might be fair to say that the apostles teaching of God's Word to His Church was the information, explanation, and application of all that Jesus had taught them while He was here on earth with them.

Wayne Grudem, in his excellent work, *The Gift of Prophecy*, devotes an entire chapter on the New Testament apostles and their authority to explain and establish the teaching of Jesus for His Church. Grudem made this observation:

> The New Testament also claims for the other apostles [other than Paul] a unique access to totally accurate information about the life and work of Christ. It is primarily the apostles who are given the ability from the Holy Spirit to recall accurately the words and deeds of Jesus and to interpret them rightly for subsequent generations."

After referring to the above passages from the Gospel of John, Grudem further explains:

Thus, the disciples are promised amazing gifts to enable them to write Scripture: the Holy Spirit would teach "all things," would cause them to remember *all* that Jesus had said, and would guide them into "all the truth."

Jesus' complete confidence in the apostles and their authority over the work of "signs and wonders" is revealed in Acts 2:43 when Luke writes, "Everyone kept feeling a sense of awe; and many wonders and signs were taking place through the apostles." In a similar passage in Acts 5:12, Luke records:

At the hands of the apostles many signs and wonders were taking place among the people; and they were all with one accord in Solomon's portico.

The authority of the apostles in the use of "signs and wonders" is further supported in 2 Corinthians 12:11b-12, when Paul defends the validity of his apostleship when he writes:

Actually I should have been commended by you, for in no respect was I inferior to the most eminent apostles, even though I am a nobody. The signs of a true apostle were performed among you with all perseverance, by signs and wonders and miracles.

It is not my purpose here to debate the Pentecostal position of signs and wonders and the miraculous. What I do want to highlight is the position of authority Jesus gave to His apostles when He went back to the Father in heaven. Their capacity to work these miracles is an extension of the signs Jesus performed on the earth to authenticate His claims to be the Son of God, the Savior of the world.

It can be legitimately argued that "signs and wonders" ended with the apostles in the same way their authoritative teaching ended with the canon of the New Testament. But it can also be argued that, while this may be true, God can move with signs and wonders with whomever and whenever He chooses.

* * *

The third major area of authority delegated to the apostles by Jesus was that of oversight for His Church. This includes:

- the collection and use of money as described in Acts 4:32-37

- standing against evil as indicated in Acts 5:1-11 and 1 Corinthians 5

- the ministry organization of the Church as seen in Ephesians 4:11-12 and Acts 6:1-6

- the expansion of the church as described in Acts 8:14-25, Acts 11:19-26, and Acts 13:1-4

Their authority was greatly needed during a major conflict in the Church, occasioned by the Judaizing heresy, as recorded in Acts 15. This prominent place of authoritative teaching, working of signs and wonders, and church oversight by the apostles is what Paul refers to in Ephesians where he explains that God's household was built on the foundation of the apostles, who were also prophets, as Wayne Grudem asserts in *The Gift of Prophecy*, with Christ Jesus Himself being the cornerstone.

So what does all this mean for today's church? I'll start grappling with that question in my next chapter.

GODLY AUTHORITY AS IT APPLIES TO THE ELDERSHIP OF THE CHURCH

When it comes to establishing authority, I've made my case that all authority has its source in God the Father, and His authority over the Church has been delegated to Jesus, the Son, who in turn delegated His authority to the apostles.

But there's one more important question to be answered about authority in the Church, and it's this: When the apostles died and went to be in the presence of the Lord, or when the Church spread beyond their jurisdiction, where did their authority then reside?

Some seminaries deal with this question in a general way when it comes to church governance and authority. They predominantly identify three forms of church government:

- episcopal

- presbyterian

- congregational

Become some seminaries and professors don't want to offend any particular denomination or tradition, they tend to imply that Scripture is not clear about this issue. This, of course, is not true of all seminaries and church leaders.

Because of this trend, though, it's safe to say that there's more confusion than clarity in many Christian institutions (churches, seminaries, and parachurch entities) about authority and how that God-ordained influence is to function biblically.

Alexander Strauch, a professor at Colorado Christian

University and author of the excellent book, *Biblical Eldership,* related a startling incident that occurred years earlier when he was taking a class on church polity while in seminary.

Since the professor teaching that class stubbornly resisted any notion of an elder-led church, Strauch raised his hand and asked him, "But what do you do with all the Scripture texts on elders?"

"The number of texts on elders means nothing!" the professor replied in an attempt to shut down any discussion on what God's Word said.

That attitude pretty much sums up where we are on the topic of church leadership. *Leadership Journal* in 2004 surveyed 506 readers who were pastors concerning conflict in their churches, and 95 percent reported having conflict at some time and 20 percent said they were currently experiencing it. What was all the ruckus about? Here's what the *Leadership Journal* article said:

> Jokes about the color of the carpet aside, the conflicts stemming from who makes the decisions is a big issue in most churches. In our survey, pastors checked all the sources of conflict from a list . . . and 85 percent of them cited control as a leading contributor. Matters of doctrine or cultural issues ranked low compared to power and personal preference. When we asked pastors to name the most likely cause, again control (44 percent) outdistanced the other factors, with vision/direction a remote second (22 percent).

Ken Sande, president of Peacemakers Ministries, cited the following statistics in an article appearing on their website:

- 23 percent of current U.S. pastors have been fired or forced to resign in the past

- 45 percent of the pastors who were fired in one denomination left the ministry altogether

- 34 percent of all pastors presently serve congregations that forced their previous pastor to resign

- the average pastoral *career* lasts only fourteen years— less than half of what it was not long ago

- 25 percent of the churches in one survey reported conflict in the previous five years that was serious enough to have a lasting impact on congregational life

- 1,500 pastors leave their assignments every month in the United States because of conflict, burnout, or moral failure

Sande went on to ask, "What is it that usually strikes pastors down? Surveys by *Christianity Today* and LeaderCare ministry revealed that the most common causes for forced exits. They were:

- the church already being conflicted when the pastor arrives

- a lack of unity and the presence of factions in the church

- conflicting visions for the church

- a church's resistance to change

- power and control struggles

- poor people skills on the part of the pastor

- conflict over leadership styles

- dissatisfaction with the pastor's performance

- theological differences

It's my firm conviction that all of these statistics point to one predominant cause: a lack of clarity about spiritual authority in the church on the part of the pastor, the lay leadership, and the congregation. This is why we need to answer the question about where the authority in the Church resides when the apostles are no longer here.

Because the authority question impacts the Church, I'd like to spend a considerable amount of time using Scripture to demonstrate how the apostles' authority transitioned to elders in the Church. This transition did not include the unique absolute authority of the apostles. That kind of authority was based on qualifications that could only have been met in the first century, as described in the first chapter of the Book of Acts. This absolute authority was given by the Holy Spirit to the apostles and later Paul. (For support of Paul's apostleship, see 1 Corinthians 15:7-9 and 2 Corinthians 12:11-12.)

Wayne Grudem is again clear and helpful in his book *The Gift of Prophecy*, writing, "These apostles had unique authority to found and govern the early church, and they could speak and write words of God. Many of their written words became the New Testament Scriptures."

To be clear about Grudem's statement, the authority of the apostles to govern the church was passed to elders. The founding of the Church and the prophetic and authoritative teaching for the Church resided only with the apostles, however.

The Development of Eldership

Now I'd like to walk you through the development of the eldership as traced in the New Testament. The word "development" is important because the word *elder* isn't always consistently used in the New Testament, but the function, role, and office become increasingly clear and refer to the position of authority delegated to these biblically qualified men.

A good place to start is in Acts 8. Due to the persecution against the church in Jerusalem following the stoning of Steven, Luke writes, "And they were all scattered throughout the regions of Judea and Samaria, except the apostles" (8:1b).

Saul, he continues, started "ravaging the church, entering house after house, and dragging off men and women" that he put into prison (8:2b). All who were scattered "went about preaching the word" (8:4b).

Philip, the deacon, traveled to Samaria and brought many to faith in the Lord Jesus. "Now when the apostles in Jerusalem heard that Samaria had received the word of God, they sent them Peter and John," says Acts 8:14. Peter and John laid hands on the new Samaritan believers so that they would receive the Holy Spirit. This was a special act of authority and shepherding by the church in Jerusalem through Peter and John.

It was especially sensitive of the Holy Spirit to lead them in this way because the Samaritans were a hated people by the Jews. God knew they needed this clear affirmation that they were also a part of the Church. At this point in the history of the early Church, spiritual authority was manifested through two of the apostles.

By comparison, look at Acts 11:21b, when the word of God has spread to Antioch where "a large number who believed turned to the Lord." Spiritual authority and care of the "church at Jerusalem" was now activated. "The news about them reached the ears of the church at Jerusalem, and they sent Barnabas off to Antioch," says Acts 11:22.

Barnabas encouraged the new believers "with resolute heart to remain true to the Lord" (verse 23), but he also realized that there was too much work for one man to do and that he needed to be part of a plurality of authority in shepherding. Barnabas then took some time from the exciting ministry at Antioch to find another shepherd/elder, who turned out to be Saul, who had been living in his hometown of Tarsus.

Barnabas was significantly instrumental in the assimilation of Saul, a relatively new believer, into the church. The point of all this is that the spiritual authority necessary to establish the church had already begun to pass from the original twelve apostles to someone else with their delegated authority.

Moving on to Acts 13, Barnabas and Saul, after teaching the congregation for "an entire year" (11:26b), met together with three more "prophets and teachers" (13:1b). These obvious leaders of the church in Antioch were taking some time "ministering to the Lord" (13:2b). One of the principles that we can learn from these chapters in Acts is is that those going to the "mission field" did not go at their own initiative. They were sent by a plurality of leadership that listened to God about His plan for the Church.

Another principle they put into place was that they did not send one man but a team of two, following the pattern of Jesus who sent out His disciples two by two in Mark 6:7. On some occasions, the team of two expanded to as many as eight, as Acts 20:4 relates.

A third principle was that you send out your best—your most mature, most gifted, most experienced—into the mission field. Paul and Barnabas were the founders of this church. When they went out proclaiming the gospel and planting churches, they knew what they were doing.

On their first missionary journey together, they didn't leave until they established spiritual, qualified authority to shepherd the flock once they departed. Here's how Acts 14:23 describes it:

> When they had appointed elders for them in
> every church, having prayed with fasting, they
> commended them to the Lord in whom they had
> believed.

This is the first time the word *elder* appears in the Acts

narrative of the expanding Church. This appointing of elders to pastor the church is also described in Paul's letter to Titus, the pastor on the island of Crete. In the first chapter, Paul explains to Titus, "For this reason I left you in Crete, that you would set in order what remains and appoint elders in every city as I directed you" (Titus 1:5).

Following their first missionary journey, a major conflict erupted for Paul and Barnabas in the church at Antioch. Acts 15:1-2 (with italics added for emphasis) explains the conflict and describes the resolution:

> Some men came down from Judea and began teaching the brethren, "Unless you are circumcised according to the custom of Moses, you cannot be saved." And when Paul and Barnabas had great dissension and debate with them, *the brethren* determined that Paul and Barnabas and some others of them should go up to Jerusalem to the apostles *and elders* concerning this issue.

The phrase "apostles and elders" is referred to again in Acts 15 in verses 4, 6, 22, and 23. At this point in the life of the early Church, the function and designation of elders was becoming more prominent and consistent.

Acts 20:17-38 is where we see how important and established the whole concept of an eldership had become in the expanding church. At this time, Paul was nearing the end of his third missionary journey and hurrying to get to Jerusalem in time for the feast of Pentecost (20:16). He didn't want to take time to stop in Ephesus, so he sent word to the elders to meet him in Miletus, about thirty-five miles southwest of Ephesus.

Paul then gives the elders a manifesto of how he has worked with them and trained them to take care of the church, followed by a powerful summary of what it means to be an elder in Acts 20:28:

> Be on guard for yourselves and for all the flock,
> among which the Holy Spirit has made you over-
> seers, to shepherd the church of God which He
> purchased with His own blood.

This key passage establishes that the authority of the apostles in overseeing the Church was transferring to the elders in the local congregations of the expanding Church.

* * *

In Acts 21:17-18, Paul and his team, including Luke, arrive at their destination in Jerusalem. As Luke's narrative records, "And the following day Paul went in with us to James, and all the elders were present" (verse 18).

What's instructive about this passage is how it refers to the leaders of the church in Jerusalem with the term *elders* only. In Acts 15 the words "apostles and elders" are used throughout. As the church expanded and the presence of the apostles became increasingly limited, though, the term *elder* was considered sufficient as a designation of church leadership and oversight. This development, however, did not indicate the fading of the apostolic presence or authority but was a clear acknowledgement that increasing numbers of the congregations were under the oversight of elders, not the apostles.

A key passage on the development of elders for newly planted churches is found in 1 Peter 5:1-4 (verse numbers included):

> ¹ Therefore, I exhort the elders among you,
> as your fellow elder and witness of the sufferings
> of Christ, and a partaker also of the glory that is
> to be revealed, ² shepherd the flock of God among
> you, exercising oversight not under compulsion,

but voluntarily, according to the will of God;
and not for sordid gain, but with eagerness; [3] nor
yet as lording it over those allotted to your charge,
but proving to be examples to the flock. [4] And
when the Chief Shepherd appears, you will
receive the unfading crown of glory.

This passage teaches many important things about elders and their place and function in the church, but I want to key in on verse 1, which states "Therefore, I exhort the elders among you, as your fellow elder and witness of the sufferings of Christ, and a partaker also of the glory that is to be revealed."

In the latter part of this verse, Peter refers to his qualification as an apostle, which is that he witnessed the sufferings of Christ. That's a convincing credential that affirms his position in the life and ministry of Jesus and now in the life of the churches. As he writes that he's sending this epistle to "those who reside as aliens, scattered throughout Pontus, Galatia, Cappadocia, Asia, and Bithynia" (1:1b), it's highly significant that he exhorts the "elders among you" in verse 1 of Chapter 5, and that their position of authority and responsibility is made clear in verses 2-4.

What I found even more significant was how Peter referred to himself as "your fellow elder" even though he designated himself as "Peter, an apostle of Jesus Christ" in his salutation in the first verse in Chapter 1.

By Chapter 5, he substitutes the title of elder for the title of apostle. This is a powerful statement of trust and affirmation of the transition of authority from apostles to elders in the growing and spreading Church of Jesus Christ. This, along with the other passages, makes it clear that the authority to oversee and care for the Church has been designated to elders.

It's difficult to understand how many Christian churches, seminaries, and leaders have failed to acknowledge this obvious truth. Christians who profess the Bible to be God's infallible Word agree that they must establish their church practices and doctrines on the teachings of the Bible. There are plenty of contemporary scholars, however, who say that the New Testament is ambiguous or silent regarding the topic of church government and conclude that no one can insist upon a biblical model of church government for all churches because the Bible doesn't.

One of those was George Eldon Ladd, author of *A Theology of the New Testament* and a professor at Fuller Theological Seminary. This is how he expressed his point of view:

> It appears likely that there was no normative pattern of church government in the apostolic age, and that the organizational structure of the church is no essential element in the theology of the church.

Although this is a widely held view among scholars today, it must be challenged because it simply does not fit the biblical evidence. Connected to this strange blindness to biblical truth about the existence and importance of eldership is a similar blindness about the qualifications for elders.

Over the years, I have frequently witnessed the highly negative effects of unqualified elders. In fact, one elder who is not qualified can immobilize the entire eldership from listening to God concerning His way for the church. When that happens, the eldership refrains from making necessary decisions and actions that God is leading them to fulfill. Having served as a senior pastor for forty-two years in one church, I can confidently state that a church led by unqualified elders is as bad or worse than having *no* elders.

I remember how at one church the governance model was mostly congregational upon my arrival and had three boards: elders, trustees, and administrative. Talk about a confused authority structure! The best I could determine, the authority was centered in the administrative board, but someone must have persuaded the church to have elders at one time.

As the senior pastor, I was an ex-officio member of all committees, including the nominating committee for these boards. There were ten of us on the committee to nominate prospective elders for a run-off congregational vote.

I remember starting the process one time with church phone directories in our hands. The first question I heard was, "Does Bill still go to our church?"

There were murmurs around the table, followed by this question: "Has he been an elder lately?"

If the answer to the first question was yes and the second was no, we put him down as a possible prospect. That's how we were vetting people.

One man was suggested who had been in the church a long time and attended faithfully, even serving in some important ministries. The previous week, this man's teenage daughter had come in to see me. She wanted to inform me that while her father seemed to be a good Christian to everyone, he really wasn't. She related how he would lose his temper if her mother prepared a meal he didn't like and throw the plate of food against the wall of the kitchen. Needless to say, I informed the committee that this man probably had some issues in his life that needed his attention before serving on the elder board.

It turned out in this process of nominating leaders to oversee the church, I was usually the only one who knew the man sufficiently to determine any qualifications. This continued my journey of distrust in congregational government that had begun ten years earlier in a small Baptist church in which I served for five years in music and youth. This church tried to take congregational government seriously and had a church-wide business meeting every month, but it usually ended in a big fight as spiritually and emotionally immature people argued about their opinions regarding the topic at hand.

So in this church where I was now the senior pastor, all the decisions about any kind of qualification were being made by me. I knew this was not right and I also knew that nobody was paying any attention to the biblical qualifications for an elder or for any leader for that matter.

As a result, the elder or administrative board never referred to Scripture when considering an issue or decision, which didn't surprise me because the meeting began with what seemed like a token prayer. Many of the pastors who had served this church before me had been seminary professors that I knew personally. They were godly men whom I respected, but they seemed oblivious to this issue of spiritual authority in the church and how it was to exist and function.

Somehow the corporate and political authority structures of our society had taken precedent over the biblical pattern, which wasn't a new problem. Alexander Strauch, in his aforementioned book, cited Jerome (circa A.D. 345-419) as declaring, "Many build churches nowadays; their walls and pillars of glowing marble, their ceilings glittering with gold, their altars studded with jewels. Yet to the choice of Christ's ministers, no heed is paid." Strauch goes on to say this:

> A similar error is repeated by multitudes of
> churches today. Many churches seem oblivious
> to the biblical requirements for their spiritual
> leaders as well as to the need for the congregation
> to properly examine all candidates for leadership
> in light of biblical standards (1 Timothy 3:10).

Gene Getz, the senior pastor at Fellowship Bible Church North in Dallas, wrote this:

> Paul viewed the position of being an "elder/overseer" as a very significant role, and anyone who had a desire to serve in this way would be pursuing a valuable, upright, and responsible ministry. However, Paul also made it unmistakably clear that a man who served in this position should demonstrate character qualities that reflect Christlike maturity.

What are some of those character qualities that Getz is talking about? I'll answer that in my next chapter.

THE QUALIFICATIONS
OF AN ELDER

A good place to start when preparing a list of qualifications for elders is God's Word, the Bible. To clarify my thoughts, I've established four categories or areas in which to consider elder qualifications:

- the first has to do with spiritual maturity and moral character

- the second is focused on spiritual gifts

- the third has to do with accessibility of the individual for the work

- and the fourth has to do with gender

That said, Paul's instructions to Timothy (1 Tim. 3:1-7) and Titus (1:5-9) provide the substance behind any discussion concerning spiritual maturity and moral character. I also want to talk about Peter's exhortation to elders in 1 Peter 5:1-4. With that out of the way, here are four areas of character qualifications for elders:

The first characteristic of a spiritually mature man is that he needs to be a committed man. This characteristic is dealt with in the context of family in both Timothy and Titus.

First of all, he is to be "a one-wife husband" or, more literally in the Greek, a "one-woman man," according to 1 Timothy 3:2a and Titus 1:6a. This phrase refers to the selection process of "having a wife." Boiled down to its essence, this means that with God's help, he has chosen one woman above all others to be his wife. He has the capacity to be attracted to many other women, but as God leads in his attraction to one single woman, he focuses his emotional, sexual, and spiritual attention on her to the exclusion of all others.

Doing so involves a commitment and a discipline of his emotions, or what C.S. Lewis refers to as "trained emotions" in his book, *The Abolition of Man.* This phrase also implies a continuous, persevering commitment and attraction to one woman. This is what enables him to hang in there when difficulties and problems arise, which they always will.

Next up, he is commanded by God to love his wife as Christ loved the Church and gave Himself up for her (Ephesians 5:25). This is not about an emotional "falling in love" and "falling out of love." Rather, it's a command that God expects him to fulfill. His commitment to God about his wife means that it's essential for his emotions to be trained only on her because marriage is the most demanding and intimate of all human relationships. If he can't live out his commitment here, he won't be able to live out his commitment to the people of his congregation—those "allotted to [his] charge" (1 Peter 5:3b).

The second major area of commitment for an elder refers to how he acts as a father to his children. He must "[keep] his children under control with all dignity" (1Timothy 3:4b). The Greek phrase used here means "having children in subjection with all gravity," according to Thayer's. This man as a father must teach, train, and model the theme of my book—submission to God and His principles of authority. To do this, he must first be submissive to the appropriate authorities in his life.

After that, he must take the time to explain to his children that God is the only Source of authority and that his authority as a father only comes from God. As discussed earlier, he must not exasperate his children to anger but must be a godly, loving authority that draws his children to reverence the principle of authority and respect him as their father in his position of authority.

If this is done with God's help and in God's way, these children will also be respectful and obedient in other relationships of authority over them. Paul refers to this qualification in his instruction to Titus about elders "having children who believe," and aren't "accused of dissipation or rebellion" (Titus 1:6b). Godly authority exercised by loving parents is a prerequisite to raising obedient, respectful, and even believing children. The man ruling his household well is a crucial qualification for being part of the "ruling" team of elders in a local church.

The second qualification area of a spiritually mature man is congeniality. One of the Greek words that describe a congenial man is that he must not be *plaktan* or "pugnacious," which means "ready with a blow, contentious, quarrelsome," according to *Thayer's*. This concept of being uncontentious is then repeated with another word. In contrast to being pugnacious and contentious, the congenial man is gentle, which has the connotation of being seemly, suitable, equitable, fair, and mild.

Another word describing a congenial man is *tuphothesis*, which is translated as "not conceited" and literally means to "raise a smoke, wrap in a mist, or to make proud to puff up with pride," according to *Thayer's*. This word is found in 1 Timothy 3:6.

Another word I want to point out—and found in Titus 1:7—is *authaoa*, which is translated "self-willed" and has expanded meanings of self-pleasing and arrogant. Any man who characteristically fails in this area of congeniality immobilizes the eldership, which will end up spending all their time dealing with this man's pride and resultant contentiousness. This will preempt all efforts at listening to God though His Word, His Spirit, and each other.

A third area of qualification for an elder is that he must be a controlled man. Several words in Timothy and Titus to describe an elder refer to being sober, abstaining from immoderate use of wine, not being addicted to wine, and not being drunken. This rather obvious qualification doesn't require a lot of explanation.

Part of being a controlled man includes his temper. This word is referred to in Titus 1:7 and simply means not being "quick-tempered, prone to anger," according to *Thayer's*. The importance of this area of control—in a man who is being evaluated as a potential elder—is powerfully referenced in Proverbs 16:32:

> He who is slow to anger is better than the mighty,
> And he who rules his spirit, than he who captures
> a city.

James writes similarly in James 1:19b-20:

> But everyone must be quick to hear, slow to
> speak and slow to anger; for the anger of man
> does not achieve the righteousness of God.

It's interesting how James connects a controlled temper with being slow to speak and quick to hear. Each of these actions require significant self-control, which is the last word used in this category of qualifications. An elder prospect must be "self-controlled," Paul writes to Titus in Titus 1:8. This qualification is also referred to in Galatians 5:23 as part of the fruit of the Spirit.

Personally, I can think back to several times in our elder meetings when I expressed myself out of frustration or anger, rather than self-control. I noticed that the other elders didn't respond to the truth I was trying to loudly convey because they didn't know how to get past my anger or frustration to the truth. This lack of control severely limits meaningful conversation and any listening to God.

One final but potent word about control is used by Paul in

writing to both Timothy (3:2) and Titus (1:8). The word is *sophrona*, translated "prudent" in Timothy and "sensible" in Titus. The Greek meanings are "of sound mind" and "curbing one's desires and impulses," according to *Thayer's*. Ability to follow these characteristics is crucial to hearing from God and obeying Him rather than advocating for your own preferences and desires. This is what frees us to follow the truth of God's Word. If your desires are out of control, then you're unable to see or respond to the truth.

This truth has amazing impact and revelatory power to understand our present-day culture, which has become, in many ways, increasingly decadent. The dominant culture of secularism and sexual liberation has been promulgated from our secular universities for decades.

E. Michael Jones has written an amazing book entitled *Degenerate Moderns*, which contains a back-cover endorsement from Ralph McInerny of the University of Notre Dame, who writes these scathing and powerful words:

> In this groundbreaking new book, Jones shows
> how some of the major determining leaders in
> modern thought and culture have rationalized
> their own immoral behavior and projected it onto
> a universal canvas. The main thesis of this book
> is that, in the intellectual life, there are only two
> ultimate alternatives: either the thinker conforms
> desire to truth or he conforms truth to desire.

I'll leave the exploration of the demise of Western culture and civilization to others, but what I want to do is highlight how crucial this concept of "curbing one's desires and impulses" is for the Church, and therefore how important this qualification is for an elder. The Church today, in my opinion, is showing signs of a significant struggle in its commitment to God's Word because of its desire to please our secular culture and make God and His Church more attractive to that culture. And that's a terrible development for the Church.

The fourth area of qualification for a spiritually mature elder is that he must be a consecrated man. There are several places where this area of qualification is referenced in Scripture. In 1 Timothy 3:3b, an elder needs to be "free from the love of money." Since money and wealth are referred to by Jesus in Matthew 6 as a prime adversary to the worship and love of God, this qualification is naturally highly important. Current church history is too often an expression of pastors' and other Christian leaders' obsession with money.

Another phrase that is used in Titus 1:7 is "not fond of sordid gain." *Sordid* refers to that which is "base, dishonorable," according to *Thayer's*. My own interpretation of this phrase includes the love of money, but also includes any manipulation of circumstances, people, or decisions for one's benefit and advantage. This can include the desire for status and power.

Another qualification in this category of consecration is "loving what is good" (Titus 1:8b). I would take this to mean that an elder is a man who loves God, loves what God is, loves what God does, and loves what God loves. This essentially means he is about God, not about the world of evil surrounding him.

In this same passage, he must be just, righteous, and passing just judgment on others. He evaluates thinking and action and people on the basis of righteousness. What this really means is an elder must be impartial in relationship to people and the decisions they make.

The last word used in this category is the word *devout*, meaning pure and holy. He must be clear about his sinfulness and the need to regularly confess and receive God's cleansing through the blood of Jesus Christ (1 John 1:5-9). In summation, an elder is all about God, His will, and His way and not about himself and his dreams and desires.

* * *

There are several other qualifications that don't necessarily fit the above four categories, so for lack of a better term, I will call them "miscellaneous."

Three words and phrases used in these Timothy and Titus passages are fairly broad and could include how those outside the Church view this man. The first specifically refers to this qualification in 1 Timothy 3:7:

> And he must have a good reputation with those outside the church, so that he will not fall into reproach and the snare of the devil.

A good reputation among those outside the Church is based upon his integrity in finances, keeping his word, and putting the needs of others ahead of his own. "Integrity in finances" means that he pays his bills on time and without complaint. It means that he isn't looking for how his Christian status can benefit him financially but rather how he can be generous and giving with others.

I have been aware of some, if not many, Christian leaders who seek and even request economic privilege or benefit from doctors or sales and service providers. This usually is in the form of asking for a discount. I prefer Abraham's attitude when the king of Sodom offered him the booty from his rescue of Lot and the Sodomites and his victory over the five Canaanite kings. Abraham said in Genesis 14:22b-23, "I have sworn to the LORD God Most High, possessor of heaven and earth, that I will not take a thread or a sandal thong or anything that is yours, for fear you would say, 'I have made Abram rich.'"

I have been amazed over the years at how just paying my bills on time with a smile has impacted unbelievers and given me a positive relationship with them. One man, who was my mechanic, called me over to introduce me to a police captain friend of his one time when I was at his shop. During his introduction, my mechanic told the police captain, "This is the most holy man I have ever met."

This was rather astounding to hear because all I had ever done was regularly use him to work on my car, which I paid right away, and inquire about how his business was doing from time to time. He must have been listening because I told him on another occasion that I was praying that God would bless him in his business.

As Christians we need to be seen as givers, not takers, especially if we are in church leadership. I have been amazed at how many unbelievers who are in business have little respect for the Christians they work with or serve. I have had some of them tell me they would never do business with a professing Christian again. I have listened to servers in restaurants tell me Christians are the worst people they serve—they complain the most, are many times rude and disrespectful, and give the worst tips.

One of the words used in 1 Timothy 3:2 is translated as "respectable." This word, *kosmion*, includes the thoughts of being "well-arranged, seemly, and modest," according to *Thayer's*, which also indicates that this word refers to a "man living with decorum, a well-ordered life." This is a related word to *kosmos*, which refers to "an apt and harmonious arrangement, order" as well as a reference to "the world, the universe."

I take this to mean that a man who elicits respect from the unbelieving world gives strong evidence of a well-ordered life in every aspect. This also reminds me of how Jesus is described in Luke 2:52 as a maturing young man:

> And Jesus kept increasing in wisdom and stature,
> and in favor with God and men.

An elder prospect must have a good reputation in the world outside the Church for these reasons:

1. **Leadership is representative.** In other words, leaders in the Church should represent to the world the Body of Christ at its best.

2. **The world is a test of truth.** A man's faith in Jesus Christ must be able to stand the test of a hostile environment and persevere under the tribulation and distress that comes to God's people (James 1:2-4).

3. **The world is a concern of God.** Their exposure to truth, light, and love is at stake. Peter said it powerfully and succinctly in this way in 1 Peter 2:12:

> Keep your behavior excellent among the
> Gentiles, so that in the thing in which they
> slander you as evildoers, they may because
> of your good deeds, as they observe them,
> glorify God in the day of visitation.

This emphasis on a good reputation for an elder in the world led those of us on the eldership board to ask for a letter from an unbelieving boss, neighbor, or relative during the elder selection process. Nothing impacts unbelievers more than a man who lives the same life of righteousness in the world during the week that he lives in the church on Sunday.

Gifting Qualifications of an Elder

Having regarded the character qualifications of an elder, it's equally important to consider his gifting qualifications. An elder's gifts have to do with how the Holy Spirit works through him in his ministry. One of those gifts is leadership, which is mentioned as one of the gifts of the Spirit by Paul in Romans 12:8, where he refers "he who leads." The word Paul uses is *prohistami*, which means "to be over, preside over, to be a protector, guardian, to care for," according to *Thayer's*.

The word *prohistami* is also used in 1 Timothy 3:4-5:

> He must be one who manages his own household
> well, keeping his children under control with
> all dignity (but if a man does not know how to
> manage his own household, how will he take care
> of the church of God?).

In addition, *prohistami* is used in 1 Timothy 5:17, where the NASB translates, "The elders who rule well are to be considered worthy of double honor, especially those who work hard at preaching and teaching."

There's another Greek word to consider, *episkopos*, which is translated as "overseer" and is a strong word indicating leadership. An overseer is "a man charged with the duty of seeing that things to be done by others are done rightly," according to *Thayer's*.

In this 1 Timothy 3 passage, the word elder is not used, only overseer— *episkopos*. In the passage about qualifications found in Titus 1, the word *overseer* and the word *elder* are used interchangeably in verses 5 and 7. *Thayer's Greek-English Lexicon* states this concerning elders:

That they did not differ at all from the bishops or overseers (acknowledged by Jerome on Titus 1:5) is evident from the fact that the two words are used indiscriminately in Acts 20:17, 28; Titus 1:5, 7, and that the duty of presbyters is described by the terms *episkopos* (to oversee) in 1 Peter 5:1-3 . . . The title *episkopos* (bishop) denotes the function, *presbuteros* (elder), the dignity; the former was borrowed from Greek institutions, the latter from the Jewish . . .

Another word used to refer to the qualification of an elder as leader is the word *poimaino*, which means "to feed, tend, keep sheep; to furnish pasturage; to rule, govern," according to *Thayer's*. This word is used in Acts 20:28 and 1 Peter 5:1-2. The *Tyndale Bible Dictionary* explains further, stating that a shepherd was:

". . . one who took complete care of a flock of sheep. His task was to find grass and water for the sheep, to protect them from wild animals (Amos 3:12), to look for and restore those that strayed (Ezekiel 34:8; Matthew 18:12), to lead the flock out of the fold each day, and to return the flock to the fold at the close of the day (John 10:2-4). For a shepherd to care for his flock he had to be completely in charge.

This is why this word moves from the metaphor of a literal shepherd to mean someone who rules or governs.

The last word to consider when thinking about an elder being qualified by his leadership gift is the word *hageomal*, which means "to go before, lead, rule command, have authority over," according to *Thayer's*. This word is found three times in Hebrews 13 in verses 7, 17, and 24. *Hageomal*, along with the other three words we have considered, presents a clear, strong concept of authority when the qualification and function of an elder are under consideration.

A second "gifting" qualification for an elder in the New Testament is that of teaching. The word used in 1 Timothy 3:2 is *didaktikon*, which means "apt and skillful in teaching," according to *Thayer's*. It's informative that this qualification is not referred to when speaking about deacons. The elder is responsible for communicating God's eternal truth in words to His people. The deacon is commissioned to serve people in their material needs.

This qualification of teaching is referred to by Paul in 1 Timothy 5:17 where he instructs:

> The elders who rule well are to be considered
> worthy of double honor, especially those who work
> hard at preaching and teaching.

"Double honor" has a financial context, but also note that the word translated "preaching" is *logos*, a comprehensive word that refers to verbal communication with words. *Logos* can mean "discourse, speech, skill and practice in speaking, continuous speaking, preaching, and instruction," according to *Thayer's*, and is connected with the word *didaskalia*, which simply means "teaching, instruction."

These words indicate that an elder must be able to speak and explain the meaning of Scripture. That this is true—in the context of the New Testament—is because teaching is always connected to God's truth. Thus an elder must be able to have a biblical ministry—the ministry of the Word (*logos*) in Acts 6:2 and Hebrews 13:7.

In his instruction to Titus (in Titus 1:9), Paul combines these words *logos* (preaching) and *didaxan* (teaching) and raises the importance of this gift for an elder. He is to be a man "holding fast the faithful word which is in accordance with the teaching, so that he may be able both to exhort in sound doctrine and to refute those who contradict."

The word for "holding fast" is *antecho*, which means to "keep oneself directly opposite to, to hold firmly, cleave to," according to *Thayer's*. An elder must be a man who has been and is assimilating God's Word into his own life. But he also must be able to disseminate that Word with exhortation of sound doctrine and even refute those that contradict that eternal Word. This gift of teaching must not be just an academic exercise but a holistic ministry that is from a total man and impacting a total man.

In Hebrews 13:7, the author encourages his readers, "Remember those who led you, who spoke the word of God to you; and considering the result of their conduct, imitate their faith." Elders must be men who live out God's Word in such an authentic way that those who have heard them teach also can follow their example.

Peter emphasizes this principle in 1 Peter 5:3 when he exhorts the elders, concerning their authority, to be "nor yet as lording it over those allotted to your charge, but proving to be examples to the flock."

What a powerful combination of words and life that God can use in the shepherding of His flock! The impact of this kind of "teaching" ministry of an elder impacts the total being of those under that teaching. Paul, again in his letters to Timothy, this time in 2 Timothy 3:16-17, glorifies this ministry when he declares:

> All Scripture is inspired by God and profitable for
> teaching, for reproof, for correction, for training
> in righteousness; so that the man of God may be
> adequate, equipped for every good work.

When considering the practical application of this crucial gift in the life of the elder, there are two important things to explain. The first is that being "able to teach" does not necessarily include any description of the configuration of the human entity receiving the teaching. Does this phrase indicate a group of one or two people, dozens, hundreds of people, or even thousands?

I refer back to 1 Timothy 5:17, when Paul writes, "The elders who rule well are to be considered worthy of double honor, especially those who work hard at preaching and teaching." This passage seems to indicate that all elders "rule" in the church, meaning they are in a position of authority, but some work hard at preaching and teaching. The fact that the qualification for all elders is that they must be able to teach is an indication that every elder must be able to understand, hold fast to, and explain the Scripture to at least one other person.

The reference to those elders who "work hard at preaching and teaching" is perhaps an indication that they are more gifted in teaching than usual and that they give more time to prepare and deliver the message of God's Word. These elders can probably communicate with a greater number of people at one time. This is an explanation of what has developed in the church over hundreds of years, which is that the pastor of a church is responsible for the majority of the preaching to a congregation. It's worthy of note that certain Reformed traditions refer to and apply this distinction of ruling elders and teaching elders.

The point I'm trying to make is that not every elder with this gift of teaching must preach to a total congregation, but he must be able to communicate God's Word into the life of at least one other individual.

I realize that there's some imprecision here, and I'm quick to admit that it's only my best effort to apply this qualification when I've been part of the process of selecting men to be elders in the local church.

* * *

A third gifting capacity for a prospective elder is that of discernment. My own understanding and thoughts about this gift include an extrapolation from the gift of teaching. If a man is gifted by God's Spirit to understand and communicate God's Word, he will very likely understand where people are in their walk with God and have a good idea of how to encourage and shepherd them.

God's Word will not only inform him about God Himself, but also about the people he is leading and shepherding. Discernment will also be developed by a leader/elder as he "keeps watch" over the souls of those allotted to his charge (Hebrews 13:17).

The word for keeping watch is *agrupneo*. Its first meaning is "to be sleepless," according to *Thayer's*. This brings to mind a characteristic of God Himself seen in Isaiah 40:27b-28, when the people of Israel have been saying: "My way is hidden from the LORD, and the justice due me escapes the notice of my God." God's reply through Isaiah is powerfully corrective:

> Do you not know? Have you not heard?
> The Everlasting God, the Lord, the Creator of the
> ends of the earth
> Does not become weary or tired.
> His understanding is inscrutable.

Another passage of Scripture that speaks of God's "sleeplessness" and attentiveness to help His people comes from Psalm 121. It's worth quoting all eight verses:

> I will lift up my eyes to the mountains;
> From where shall my help come?
> My help comes from the Lord,
> Who made heaven and earth.
> He will not allow your foot to slip;
> He who keeps you will not slumber.
> Behold He who keeps Israel
> Will neither slumber nor sleep.

The LORD is your keeper;
The LORD is your shade on your right hand.
The sun will not smite you by day,
Nor the moon by night.
The LORD will protect you from all evil;
He will keep your soul.
The LORD will guard your going out and your
coming in
From this time forth and forever.

I return to *Thayer's* description of *agrupneo,* which also means "to exercise constant vigilance over something." When a shepherd watches his sheep with this kind of vigilance, he gets to know his sheep and to discern what is going on with them and what he needs to do for them.

The connection to Jesus' teaching is remarkable. "I am the good shepherd, and I know My own and My own know Me," He said in John 10:14. We cannot come close to attributing to an elder—a human, after all—the power and wisdom of Jesus Himself for His sheep, but we can say with confidence that Jesus intends for an elder to take on an amazing responsibility of care for His sheep. His diligent vigilance in watching the sheep allotted to his charge will provide him with the discernment he needs to "keep watch over [their] souls" (Heb. 13:17b).

The writer of the book of Hebrews intensifies this responsibility when he adds, "as those who will give an account" in Hebrews 13:17c. That elders will give an account to Jesus, the Chief Shepherd, is affirmed by Peter in 1 Peter 5:2-4 in which he exhorts elders to:

> . . . shepherd the flock God among you . . . those
> allotted to your charge. . . and when the Chief
> Shepherd appears, you will receive the unfading
> crown of glory.

Too many times in our churches, elders are looked on as part of an organizational structure that could be implemented much as you would a corporation or a political party. In reality, elders have been supernaturally assigned by Jesus Himself to care for *His* sheep.

These qualifications, both in spiritual character and Spirit gifting, are indispensable for a man to fulfill this assignment. An elder may by gifted by the Holy Spirit in other ways, but these three gifts—leading, teaching, and discernment—are absolutely necessary. Without them, he will be unable to shepherd God's church with the authority Jesus has given him.

Practical Qualification of an Elder

One area of qualification that has nothing to do with moral character or spiritual gifting is that of accessibility. These are questions that have be asked among the elder board:

- Does this man have the time in his schedule to give to the oversight of the church?

- Is his work so demanding in this season of his life that he cannot add this responsibility without doing harm to himself or to his family?

- Are his children and his wife in a season of their lives where he should give full attention to them as his first priority in ministry?

- Is his health sufficiently strong to provide the energy he will need to serve in this capacity?

Make no mistake, serving as an elder is highly demanding. In fact, the Scripture is clear that an elder is expected to work hard, and his leadership is to be exercised "with diligence" (Romans 12:8b).

This word "diligence" indicates being in a hurry. It speaks of intense effort. It is the same word used in Ephesians 4:3 to exhort us to be diligent to keep the unity of the Spirit in the bond of peace.

"Earnestness" would be a synonym that leads *Thayer's* to define it as "earnestness in accomplishing, promoting, or striving after anything." It is the opposite of careless or even casual.

Paul, in his first epistle to the Thessalonians, asks them to "appreciate those who diligently labor among you, and have charge over you in the Lord and give you instruction (admonish you)" in 1 Thessalonians 5:12b. The word translated here—"diligently labor"—means "to labor with wearisome effort."

This a present active participle that indicates continuous action. In fact, picture a mother of small children who is watching them, caring for them, and training them constantly throughout the day—and sometimes throughout the night! In a similar manner, this also describes the attention and work of elders who constantly are watching over the souls of their people—their flock.

Another part of accessibility has to do with the candidate's willingness. Peter, in 1 Peter 5:2, deals very specifically with this important qualification as he exhorts the elders of the target churches:

> . . . shepherd the flock of God among you, exercising oversight not under compulsion, but voluntarily, according to the will of God; and not for sordid gain, but with eagerness.

There are several crucial points that Peter is emphasizing that are amazingly relevant to how churches select their elders. The first thing he states is that the candidate must not be considering this responsibility "under compulsion." This word *compulsion* connotes doing something by force or constraint.

In my experience, this constraint can be fueled by a constitutional requirement to have a certain number of elders. The nominating committee is faced with the task of coming up with enough candidates to eventually, after a vote of the congregation, arrive at the designated number. Pressure is usually placed on candidates to "do your part," or "you only have to serve for three years," or "the other people have done it too much already," or any other kind of manipulative platitude.

The pressure can also come from a wife who wants her husband to have a position of status in the church, which I recall happened one time. It's much preferable when the elder candidate responds to the prompting of the Holy Spirit working through his own will. He needs to be sure God is leading him to take on this critical role in the building of God's Church.

Again, I refer to Alexander Strauch's helpful book, *Biblical Eldership*, in which he writes:

> A true desire to lead the family of God is always a Spirit-generated desire. Paul reminded the Ephesian elders that it was the Holy Spirit—not the church or the apostles—who placed them as overseers in the church to shepherd the flock of God (Acts 20:28). It was the Spirit who called them to shepherd the church and who moved them to care for the flock.
>
> The Spirit planted the pastoral desire in their hearts. He gave the compulsion and strength to do the work and the wisdom and appropriate gifts to care for the flock. The elders were His wise choice for the task. In the church of God, it is not man's will that matters but God's will and arrangement.

On a few occasions over the years, I have witnessed men wanting to "put on the uniform and wear the badge." It was obvious that the status of leadership was desired by them. That is not a "true desire to lead the family of God."

Elder candidates have to want the job for the right reasons. Peter states that a candidate's willingness is not to be tepid and reluctant, but "with eagerness." This literally means he is ready, willing, and cheerful to assume this role.

Paul, in 1 Timothy 3:1, instructs in a similar tone:

> It is a trustworthy statement: if any man aspires
> to the office of overseer, it is a fine work he
> desires to do.

The word *aspire* is strong. It literally means "to stretch one's self out in order to grasp something," according to *Thayer's*. The second word—*desire*—is another strong word that refers to emotion and passion that is "turned upon a thing." In this context, the word refers to the role and responsibility of an elder.

To sum up what it means to become an elder: he is so moved by God's Spirit that he sees it as the will of God to take on this ministry and he eagerly, cheerfully, and passionately longs to do so.

To have men who possess these biblical qualifications leading our churches is a tremendous encouragement to our people and gives glory to our God. To have men leading the Church who do not qualify before God in this way will be disastrous for the Church and a reproach on the name of Christ, the Head of the Church.

I've been talking exclusively about men becoming elders and the qualifications they need to bring with them. Can women serve in leadership on elder boards? I'll tackle that topical question in my next chapter.

15

THE GENDER OF AN ELDER

I now wade into a sinkhole of controversy and polarization in the Church, and it's whether women can become elders on a leadership team. The issue of women serving on the elder team—or as pastors, for that matter—has sadly become a source of division within the Church.

Let me be as clear I can be: in terms of gender qualification, Scripture is abundantly straightforward and unambiguous—an elder must be male. It would defy logic and deny the context of the entirety of Scripture to state otherwise. Having laid out my cards on the table, I feel that it's important to take some time in the Scriptures to validate this teaching.

The Male Headship Principle in Both the Home and the Church

To begin with, the clear teaching in the Scripture about male headship in the home (which I described in Chapter 5) provides a foundation for male headship in the Church. It would be silly and ignore common sense to promote male headship in the home and deny it in the Church. There is confusion in many quarters, however, especially when male headship is so clearly connected to Jesus being the head of the Church (Ephesians 5:23-24). Vern Poythress, a professor of New Testament interpretation at Westminster Theological Seminary, ably defends this thesis in his chapter entitled "The Church as Family" in *Recovering Biblical Manhood and Womanhood*.

His summary statement of an extended argument reads as follows:

> The leadership within a family is vested in the husband and father (Ephesians 5:22-6:4). The church as God's household also needs wise and competent leadership. That leadership is to be sought among men who have already shown their abilities in the context of their immediate families (1Timothy 3:1-7).
>
> Women, by contrast, are not to be placed in authority in the church, because such a role would not harmonize with the general relations between men and women in marriage, as established at creation (1Timothy 2:11-14). Thus, the differences between men and women within the context of marriage and family carry over into differences in roles that men and women may assume within the church.

The qualification of the male gender as an elder is further substantiated by the selection by Jesus of twelve men as apostles. Even though the apostles were equipped in ways that no elders are today, the apostles are the prototype for elders concerning the issue of authority, as discussed previously. What I want to build on is that when Judas was replaced in Acts 1, it would have been an opportune time to appoint a woman in leadership, especially Mary, the mother of Jesus. She was arguably the most godly, loving, and experienced woman among God's people. She was not appointed, however, and it wasn't because of any moral or spiritual defects. The reason she wasn't asked is obvious: she was a woman, and God does not want a woman to be in this place of authority.

Therefore, the two candidates put forward by the apostles—Joseph (called Barsabbas) and Matthias—were both men. This did not happen by accident or because the men making the choice thought that women were inferior to them. Instead, it happened because this was God's order and pattern for male/female relationships that has been consistently present in all of Scripture.

This brings me to relate a pivotal passage in the New Testament that summarizes and declares this principle and pattern of God's order. This entire passage from 1 Timothy 2:8-15, with verse numbers, is greatly determinative in establishing this truth:

> [8] Therefore I want the men in every place to pray, lifting up holy hands, without wrath and dissension.
>
> [9] Likewise, I want women to adorn themselves with proper clothing, modestly and discreetly, not with braided hair and gold or pearls or costly garments, [10] but rather by means of good works, as is proper for women making a claim to godliness. [11] A woman must quietly receive instruction with entire submissiveness. [12] But I do not allow a woman to teach or exercise authority over a man, but to remain quiet. [13] For it was Adam who was first created, and then Eve. [14] And it was not Adam who was deceived, but the woman being deceived, fell into transgression. [15] But women will be preserved through the bearing of children if they continue in faith and love and sanctity with self-restraint.

In the first four verses of 1 Timothy 2, Paul urges the Church to pray for men in all walks of life with "entreaties and prayers, petitions and thanksgivings" (2:1b). The purpose of these prayers was that the Church would become part of God's desire for "all men to be saved and to come to the knowledge of the truth" (2:4b). The phrase "all men" includes women, of course.

In verses 5 and 6, Paul succinctly summarizes the gospel message: There is one true God and one Mediator between that God and men. This Mediator opens the door for a relationship of sinful man with a holy God. The Mediator is none other than "the man Christ Jesus, who gave Himself as a ransom for all" (2:5b-6a).

In verse 7, Paul identifies himself as a preacher and apostle to the Gentiles "in faith and truth." In his emphasis on the gospel, Paul reminds Timothy that the major purpose of the Church is to bring the gospel to a lost world, thereby rescuing sinners from the powers of darkness. Paul then returns to the emphasis he made in the first four verses of this chapter and clarifies how both men and women will be part of this process.

It is clear from verse 8 that God wants men to lead in this battle for the souls of men. Paul, writing under the inspiration of the Holy Spirit, declares, "Therefore I want the men in every place to pray, lifting up holy hands, without wrath and dissension."

In this summary of what God expects of men in this battle, the first thing Paul wants them to give attention to is prayer because the essence of prayer is dependence on God. Prayer is where you start in the battle. It is an expression of inadequacy, even helplessness. It's the way you get past saying, "I can't do it. It is too much."

Prayer is also the way you avoid thinking that you can win the battle on your own. Prayer is the way you connect to the power of the Holy Spirit.

The power of the Holy Spirit is important. The apostles were commanded by Jesus before He ascended, in in Acts 1:4b-5:

> . . . not to leave Jerusalem, but to wait for what
> the Father had promised, "Which," He said, "you

heard of from Me; for John baptized with water, but you will be baptized with the Holy Spirit not many days from now."

Jesus also said this in Acts 1:8:

" . . . but you will receive power when the Holy Spirit has come upon you; and you shall be My witnesses both in Jerusalem, and in all Judea and Samaria, and even to the remotest part of the earth."

After ten days of waiting and praying in the upper room, the Holy Spirit came with power to baptize and indwell the apostles and all who were with them.

Notice that God wanted men to wage this war through leadership in holiness. They were to lift up "holy" hands. The Greek word for holy is *hosious*, which means "undefiled by sin, free from wickedness, observing every moral obligation, pure, pious, and free," according to *Thayer's*, and "freedom from ungodly thought and action," according to *Kittel*.

One way to understand God's desire for holiness in our lives is by knowing that He wants us to stand with Him against evil and win over evil in our own lives. We can only do this with the power of His Spirit (Romans 8:1-4) and the confession of our sin when we fail (1 John 1:5-9).

When I say that God wants men to lead in this battle against evil, I in no way am excluding women. They need to be with the men in the battle. What I am saying, though, is that this passage clearly indicates that men are to be on the "front lines" in this battle.

I refer you to two narratives in the Old Testament that set this pattern of men being in the "front lines." I'll start with revisiting God's creation of man and woman and their subsequent disobedience and resultant fall impacting the entire human race.

God made man first and placed him in the Garden with only one prohibition: *Don't eat of the tree of the knowledge of good and evil, or you will surely die.*

It was Adam's responsibility to obey God and to lead Eve to obey God, after God had brought her to him. This he failed to do, and then he gave in to Eve's leadership in eating the fruit of that tree. That this narrative is true is validated by God Himself after they both had eaten and the sentence of death began its terrible work in their lives.

The separation that death brings began with Adam and Eve hiding "themselves from the presence of the LORD" in Genesis 3 (verse 8b). Even though Eve initiated the disobedience, the Scripture is clear whom God held responsible: "Then the LORD God called to the man and said to him 'Where are you?'" (3:9). Then God, after some revealing dialogue, said to Adam, "Have you eaten from the tree of which I commanded you not to eat?" (3:11b).

Later, in establishing the consequences of Adam's disobedience, God said in Genesis 3:17b:

> "Because you have listened to the voice of your
> wife, and have eaten from the tree about which I
> commanded you, saying, 'You shall not eat from
> it';
> Cursed is the ground because of you . . ."

One would have to ignore the plain reading of this narrative not to conclude that God expected Adam to lead his wife in the battle against evil, which is why He held him accountable for that failure.

Based on the first three chapters of Genesis, Ray Ortlund succinctly defined the man's leadership by writing, "In the partnership of two spiritually equal human beings, man and woman, the man bears the primary responsibility to lead the partnership in a God-glorifying direction." Then Ortlund drove this truth home in this comment regarding the mutual failure of Adam and Eve to obey God's clear, simple command:

> But if Adam and Eve fell into sin together, why does Paul blame Adam for our fall in Romans 5:12-21? Why doesn't Paul blame both Adam and Eve? Why does Genesis 3:7 say that it was only after Adam joined in the rebellion that the eyes of both of them were opened to their condition? Why does God call out to Adam, "Where are you?" (Genesis 3:9)? Why doesn't God summon both Adam and Eve to account together? Because, as the God-appointed head, Adam bore the primary responsibility to lead their partnership in a God-glorifying direction.

Another narrative in Scripture that emphasizes male leadership in holiness and the battle against evil is the establishment of the Abrahamic and Old Testament Covenant with circumcision as the "sign" of that covenant. I have to confess that for much of my life, I only thought of circumcision as a hygienic, medical procedure executed on our two infant sons. I never gave much thought to the institution of circumcision established by God with Abraham as revealed in Genesis 17 until I came to that chapter while I was preaching through Genesis one time.

One of the reasons I'm an advocate of pastors preaching through books of the Bible is that you are forced to deal with the things God has revealed without human selective preferences. On this occasion, I ended up teaching for four Sundays just on the subject of circumcision! I described how God initiated His covenant with Abram in Genesis 12 and 15 and then in 17, how He described the covenant more completely in verses 1-8. Then in verses 9-14, God establishes circumcision as the "sign" of the covenant, saying in verses 9b-11:

> "Now as for you, you shall keep My covenant, you and your descendants after you throughout their generations. This is My covenant, which you shall keep, between Me and you and your descendants after you: every male among you shall be circumcised. And you shall be circumcised in the flesh of your foreskin, and it shall be the sign of the covenant between Me and you."

After requiring servants, born or bought, also to be circumcised, God indicates the seriousness of this sign of the covenant in verse 14 when He warns, "But an uncircumcised male who is not circumcised in the flesh of his foreskin, that person shall be cut off from his people; he has broken My covenant." The covenant speaks much of establishing Abraham's descendants as a "multitude of nations" (verses 4-6) and the land as an "everlasting possession" (verse 8).

The heart of the covenant, however, is made clear in Genesis 17:1b where God says to Abram (changed to Abraham in verse 5):

> "I am God Almighty;
> Walk before Me, and be blameless."

God re-emphasizes this in verse 7 when He refers to the covenant as an everlasting covenant "between Me and you and your descendants after you," and again in verse 8 referring to the "land of Canaan, for an everlasting possession; and I will be [your descendants'] God." This covenant is a covenant of faith and is designed to bring Abraham and his descendants (including us as followers of Jesus) into a relationship with God Himself that is characterized by holiness. This is because God is absolutely, infinitely holy. The amazing truth is that He wants us to share in His holiness in an eternal relationship with Him.

This purpose and covenant of God is expressed multiple times throughout the Scriptures. God's covenant with Abraham was extended to the nation of Israel under the leadership of Moses just prior to God giving the Ten Commandments on Mount Sinai in Exodus 19:3-6a:

> Moses went up to God, and the LORD called to him
> from the mountain, saying, "Thus you shall say to
> the house of Jacob and tell the sons of Israel: 'You
> yourselves have seen what I did to the Egyptians,
> and how I bore you on eagles' wings, and brought
> you to Myself. Now then, if you will indeed obey
> My voice and keep My covenant, then you shall
> be My own possession among all the peoples,
> for all the earth is Mine; and you shall be to Me
> a kingdom of priests and a *holy nation*.'" (with
> italics added for emphasis).

In the Book of Leviticus, the word "holy" appears ninety times. In the midst of all the offerings and regulations, all designed to elevate God's concern for holiness, God spoke these words to His people in Leviticus 11:44a,45:

> "For I am the Lord your God. Consecrate your-
> selves therefore, and be holy, for I am holy. . . For
> I am the Lord who brought you up from the land
> of Egypt to be your God; thus you shall be holy,
> for I am holy."

This message is repeated in Leviticus 19:2 and 20:7. In Ephesians 1:3-4a Paul reveals this glorious purpose as fulfilled in Jesus Christ:

> Blessed be the God and Father of our Lord Jesus
> Christ, who has blessed us with every spiritual
> blessing in the heavenly places in Christ, just as

He chose us in Him before the foundation of the world, that we would be *holy and blameless* before Him [with italics added for emphasis].

Similarly, Peter joins this repeated message of God's Word in 1 Peter 1:14-16:

As obedient children, do not be conformed to the former lusts which were yours in your ignorance, but like the Holy One who called you, be holy yourselves also in all your behavior; because it is written, "YOU SHALL BE HOLY, FOR I AM HOLY [with italics added for emphasis].

It's been enlightening to me to understand God's holiness as an attribute that defines His relationship to evil. We know from Scripture that:

- He hates evil (Psalm 5:5, Proverbs 6:16-18, and Romans 1:18).

- He is never tempted by evil (James 1:13).

- He is totally separated from evil (1 John 1:5).

- He cannot even look at evil (Habakkuk 1:13).

- He always wins against evil (2 Timothy 4:18, 1 John 5:18, and Matthew 6:13).

- And someday He will destroy all evil (Revelation 19:11-20:15).

Theologian G. R. Lewis in his article, "God, Attributes of" in the *Evangelical Dictionary of Theology*, writes the following statement on this subject:

God is distinct from and transcendent to all his

creatures, not only metaphysically and epistemo-
logically, but also morally. God is morally spotless in character and action, upright, pure, and
untainted with evil desires, motives, thought,
words, or acts. God is *holy*, and as such is the
source and standard of what is right. God is free
from all evil, loves all truth and goodness. He
values purity and detests impurity and inau-
thenticity. God cannot approve of any evil, has no
pleasure in evil (Psalm 5:4), and cannot tolerate
evil (Habakkuk 1:13). God abhors evil and cannot
encourage sin in any way (James 1:13-14).

The Hebrew word in the Old Testament used most often for
the English word "holy" is *qadhosh. Nelson's New Illustrated
Bible Dictionary* defines the word as "moral, ethical wholeness,
or perfection; freedom from moral evil."

Thomas E. McComiskey, in his article in the *Theological
Wordbook of the Old Testament*, expands on this thought:

Because God is holy, He is free from the moral
imperfections and frailties common to man (Hosea
11:9) and can be counted on to be faithful to His
promises (Psalm 22:3-5) . . . The title "The Holy
One of Israel" is applied to God numerous times
in the OT, but is especially frequent in the prophecy of Isaiah (in all parts). It serves to place the
sins of Isaiah's society in stark contrast to God's
moral perfection (Isaiah 30:11) and expresses
God's absolute separation from evil (Isaiah 17:7).

The Greek word mostly translated "holy" in the New Testament
is *hagios*. One of its meanings, according to *Thayer's*, is "to be
set apart for God, as it were, exclusively His." Another meaning

especially germane to this discussion is, again from *Thayer's*, "to be pure, sinless, upright, holy." As I've attempted to make my case regarding holiness in God as an attribute that describes His relationship to evil, I can confidently say that His desire is for us to stand against evil and win over evil.

This intention of God is declared in the disciple's prayer that Jesus taught in Matthew 6:13a. We are to pray to the Father that He will "not lead us into temptation, but deliver us from evil." This is to be our desire as well and commitment to stand with Him against all evil and to ask for His help to win over all evil.

This leads me to return to the subject of circumcision. The heart of God's covenant with Abraham and all His people is that we should be in a loving relationship with Him that is characterized by holiness. The sign of this covenant in the Old Testament with Abraham and the nation of Israel was circumcision. In a defining way, circumcision conveyed Abraham's and the nation of Israel's commitment to holiness, to standing against evil, and to winning over evil. This covenant was a reminder to the children of Israel that they had a specific way to be serious about winning over evil. The covenant provided a process that prepared their hearts to respond to God's call to holiness.

* * *

There are two important questions to ask about circumcision:

1. Why did God mandate a sign that only applied to males?

2. Why did God's sign, manifested only in males, involve their sexuality?

The answer to the first question is that, as in the beginning with Adam, God expects the male species of the human race to take the lead in the battle against evil. The answer to the second question is that God wants male sexuality to be a priority where men win over evil. This is because so much evil has been manifested by men in their sexual treatment of women throughout the history of the human race. It is also because men have used their sexuality as a powerful expression of self-centeredness that has hindered and sometimes destroyed their relationship to God.

God has shown Himself to be highly concerned about this whole issue of circumcision. When God sent Moses to Egypt to confront Pharaoh about the evil of his oppression of the children of Israel and his arrogant rebellion against God, He challenged Moses on the trip in what seems to be a rather bizarre incident. The recording of this incident is in Exodus 4:24-26:

> Now it came about at the lodging place on the way that the LORD met him and sought to put him to death. Then Zipporah took a flint and cut off her son's foreskin and threw it at Moses' feet, and she said, "You are indeed a bridegroom of blood to me." So He let him alone. At that time she said, "You are a bridegroom of blood"—because of the circumcision.

Apparently, Moses had been reminded of the Lord's covenant with Abraham and its sign of circumcision. It would also seem that Zipporah, Moses' wife, had resisted her husband's efforts to explain this sign and carry it out with their young son. This is probably due to the nurturing, compassionate, and protective heart God has placed in all women.

That wonderful gift God had given to her, however, must bow before God's sovereign will and purposes. Zipporah's willfulness and Moses' giving in to her was not tolerated by the Lord. The statement that He sought to put him to death is an indication that Moses had put pleasing his wife above being obedient to his

God. It is also an indication that Moses wouldn't be able to fulfill God's command to confront Pharaoh and stand against all that evil if he was not standing against the evil in his own household.

Another major event that took place that reveals God's insistence that men lead their families in standing against evil is recorded in the fifth chapter of Joshua. Before beginning their conquest of the Canaanites, God commanded Joshua to circumcise all the "sons of Israel the second time" (verse 2b).

The men who had come out of Egypt had been circumcised, but because of their disobedience in refusing to go in and fight for the Promised Land, they had all died in the wilderness during the forty years of wandering the desert. The new generation of men who were ready to fight had never been circumcised. So "their children whom He raised up in their place, Joshua circumcised; for they were uncircumcised, because they had not circumcised them along the way," says verse 7.

This is a dramatic enforcement of God's insistence that the children of Israel renew their covenant with God through enacting the sign of the covenant—circumcision. They were going into physical battle, but more importantly, they were being sent by God to engage the forces of darkness in spiritual warfare. He would not let them take on this mission without reminding them that spiritual warfare against evil began in their own lives.

As I've already stated, this does not mean women are excluded from this battle, but what it does mean is that God wants men on the front lines. This is why, in 1 Timothy 2:8, the Holy Spirit through Paul begins with men lifting holy hands in prayer when the congregation gathers for worship. This focus on the men is an important indication that men are to be in the front line of action when it comes to authority and responsibility in the Church, which includes eldership.

So what *are* the roles and responsibilities women should have in the Church? I'll tackle this timely question in my next chapter.

16

ROLES AND RESPONSIBILITIES FOR WOMEN IN THE CHURCH

I now come to the responsibility of women in the Church's mission and battle against the forces of darkness to bring salvation through Jesus Christ to a lost world. From my study, there are three areas of activity and responsibility that God desires for women in the Church:

- The first is to avoid a major distraction.

- A second is to exhibit a spiritual passion.

- And a third is to embrace her godly calling.

The major distraction for women to avoid is dealt with by Paul in 1 Timothy 2:9:

> Likewise, I want women to adorn themselves
> with proper clothing, modestly and discreetly,
> not with braided hair and gold or pearls or costly
> garments.

Without taking the time to unpack all these words and phrases, I will make several summary statements about this directive and address them to women:

1. **Let the beauty of your outward appearance be well-arranged and well-ordered as God has done in creation.** Embrace and maximize how God has made you.

2. **Let the beauty of your outward appearance turn people toward God, not away from Him.** Develop a

healthy, godly sense of modesty. There is something going on that is bigger than you, and you don't want to hinder it in any way. Avoid extravagance, which leads to materialism, and avoid enticement, which leads to sexual lust.

3. **Let the beauty of your outward appearance be ordered by a heart and mind that is characterized by self-control and common sense based on God's call on your life.** God's call and presence in our lives leads us to curb our own desires in order to fulfill His. Let your planning and creating of beauty include God.

My summary of all three statements goes like this: God has called you as a woman to be involved in the battle against evil. Along with the men, you need to be part of our public prayers and united efforts for the salvation of sinners. Let Him use your physical appearance as an asset to that call, not a liability.

The second major area of responsibility and activity for women in the Church is exhibiting a spiritual passion. This is indicated in 1 Timothy 2:10 where Paul exhorts women to have spiritual passion as a meaningful contrast to the distorted emphasis on physical appearance in verse 9. As Paul says in verse 10, "but rather by means of good works, as is proper for women making a claim to godliness."

Don't allow the brevity of this verse to minimize its importance. In Ephesians 2:10, Paul highlights the importance of good works as he declares:

> For we are His workmanship, created in Christ Jesus for good works, which God prepared beforehand so that we would walk in them.

Jesus speaks the same in Matthew 5:16:

> Let your light shine before men in such a way
> that they may see your good works, and glorify
> your Father who is in heaven.

"Good works" is a phrase that encompasses the entire work of God's Spirit in and through the Church and in the world. Women are to be fully part of this great work of God without limitation, except in the area of authority, which is explained in the remaining verses of 1 Timothy 2 (verses11-15). The application of verses 9 and 10 go like this: Don't let Satan or our confused, pathetic culture define you as a woman, based on your physical beauty. And certainly—especially if you're a young woman—don't allow narcissistic, self-absorbed, hormone-driven males to have any say about who you are. Let God define you as His child and His servant to proclaim His glory in a broken, dark, and dying world.

I will never forget one of the godliest women I have ever known. Her name was Beaulah Simpson, and she was an unmarried missionary that our little neighborhood church supported in a ministry outreach to the poor in Southern California, at a location the residents referred to as a "camp." I decided, as the young pastor of this little church I was leading, that I should become acquainted with Miss Simpson. So one afternoon, I drove twenty-five or so miles to the "camp" where she lived. Her residence turned out to be a small, dusty little cottage needing repair and paint.

When I knocked on the door, an older woman with long straggly hair, mixed with gray and yellow, greeted me. Her name was Beaulah Simpson, and her dress was old and worn. I told her who I was and that I had come to get acquainted with her and her ministry.

In the course of our conversation, she opened a photo album and showed me pictures of children and families in great need that she had taken in to live with her over the many years she had been in this camp-like barrio. She ended by pointing to a picture of a girl she had not only taken in to live with her but had adopted. (Some years later, I had the privilege of marrying that wonderful young woman to a fine young Christian man. My wife, Grace, played the piano for the wedding.)

After spending several hours with Miss Simpson, I wept most of the way home. The awareness of this woman's lack of a husband, her total unconcern about herself and her poverty and lowly circumstances moved me deeply. In addition, my awareness of how God used Miss Simpson to minister in such loving and selfless abandon overwhelmed me as well. Her years of good works had made her lowly appearance and her difficult circumstances irrelevant.

I'm not trying to say that lowly appearance and meager living conditions should be the goal for any woman. What I'm saying is that a life that is passionate about good works in a biblical sense is what godliness is all about. It will be a privilege for me to share the glory of heaven in God's presence with Beaulah Simpson some day.

The third area of responsibility for women in the Church is that of embracing her godly calling. This begins with her being a fully recognized member of the Body of Christ. Along with the men, she is to "receive instruction" in God's truth through His Word, as 1 Timothy 2:11 describes.

The word translated "receive instruction" means "to learn, be apprised, to increase in knowledge," according to *Thayer's*. This clearly infers she is as capable of understanding and living her life according to the Word of God as any man. There is an equality of male and female in their relationship to God and in their value, importance, and position before Him. As Galatians 3:28-29 says:

> There is neither Jew nor Greek, there is neither
> slave nor free man, there is neither male nor

female; for you are all one in Christ Jesus. And
if you belong to Christ, then you are Abraham's
descendants, heirs according to promise.

Returning to 1 Timothy 2:11, this verse indicates an attitude by which a woman is to learn. This attitude is based on the role God has given her to support and respect the place of authority God has assigned to her husband, if married, and men in general, if single. She obviously does not submit to men in general in the same way women submit to their husbands, but in the context of the Church gathered for worship in this passage, the role of men and women in general is in view.

That role, as has been previously indicated, is part of the overview of authority relationships given in 1 Corinthians 11:3:

But I want you to understand that Christ is the
head of every man, and the man is the head of a
woman, and God is the head of Christ.

This passage would seem to be referring to man and woman in a general sense, as is true of the 1 Timothy 2 passage. Biblical scholar Thomas R. Schreiner states that "most scholars detect a reference to men and women in general" and later states, concerning its usage in verse 11, that the singular "woman" should not be limited to an individual woman and the alternation from the plural "women" in verses 9-10 to the singular "woman" in verses 11-12 reveals that the latter is generic and all women are included.

In his chapter in *Recovering Biblical Manhood and Womanhood*, Schreiner writes that in 1 Corinthians 11:2-16 "Paul does not forbid women to participate in public worship, yet he does insist that in their participation they should evidence a demeanor that is humble and submissive to male leadership." The reason I have taken the time to emphasize this issue of men and women relating to each other in terms of authority is because these two texts indicate that. But I also want to include single women and men in this discussion. They do not lose their sexuality because they are not married. God's order of authority in relationship to men and women includes *all* men and *all* women.

Returning to the passage in 1 Timothy 2:11, Paul writes, "A woman must quietly receive instruction with entire submissiveness." Particularly in our current rebellious society and culture this sounds, at best, highly insensitive, and at worse, inflammatory and hopelessly outdated. The emphasis of this passage is not silence, as in "keep your mouth shut." The emphasis of the word *quiet* includes peacefulness and rest.

This would mean that the woman is to be a full part of the learning process with a quiet spirit. This is based on her submission to God's order in terms of her relationship to her husband. In other words, learning the full truth of God's Word was completely encouraged by Paul. In fact, this whole phrase used by Paul is an imperative and a command, not a request for permission.

Some may ask the question, *Why this emphasis on quietness and submission in regard to a woman learning God's truth?* Thomas R. Schreiner asserts, "That women should learn is undoubtedly commended, and yet the central concern is the manner in which they learn." A quiet spirit and submission to the authority of God through her husband is to characterize a woman in all aspects of her life. One thing Paul was doing was correcting the distortion of rabbinic teaching that limited a woman in her learning. He was also affirming the high calling of a woman in relationship to her husband as God has given it to her. Her submission also includes the male leaders who are teaching her.

Schreiner again is helpful when he adds, "Women were to learn with entire submissiveness from the men who had authority in the church and manifested that authority through their teaching." Learning God's truth in quietness and all submissiveness is embracing the rest and peace that comes from living her life submissively in the church as well as in the home "as to the Lord" (Ephesians 5:22b).

* * *

We now arrive at the most controversial section of this pivotal passage—1 Timothy 2:12-15, which I will repeat here because of its importance to the discussion (with verse numbers included):

> [12] But I do not allow a woman to teach or exercise authority over a man, but to remain quiet. [13] For it was Adam who was first created, and then Eve. [14] And it was not Adam who was deceived, but the woman being deceived, fell into transgression. [15] But women will be preserved through the bearing of children if they continue in faith and love and sanctity with self-restraint.

Douglas Moo of Trinity Evangelical Divinity School maintains that women have been given spiritual gifts to minister in the church. He further contends that "their ministries are indispensable to the life and growth of the church." Moo then asks the question, "Does the New Testament place any restrictions on the ministry of women?"

In answering that question, he reveals how important this passage from 1 Timothy is to our understanding of this crucial issue:

> We think 1 Timothy 2:8-15 imposes two restrictions on the ministry of women: they are not to teach Christian doctrine to men and they are not to exercise authority directly over men in

the church. These restrictions are permanent and authoritative for the church in all times and places and circumstances as long as men and women are descended from Adam and Eve.

Paul's use of quietness and submission to characterize a woman's process of learning God's truth leads him into a clear prohibition of women in a place of spiritual authority over men in the context of the Church. This prohibition includes teaching in the public gathering of the church for worship when men are present. It obviously does not include her teaching other women or her children since Paul in Titus 2:3-5 specifically instructs older women to "[teach] what is good" to the younger women.

Paul then goes on to expand their teaching to "encourage the young women to love their husbands, to love their children, to be sensible, pure, workers at home, kind, being subject to their own husbands, that the word of God may not be dishonored." A woman is prohibited, therefore, from exercising authority over a man and continues to be encouraged "to remain quiet." The substance of these prohibitions is that a woman is not to resist or circumvent God's established order of male authority in the church. This she would be guilty of doing if she taught men in any biblically authoritative way or exercised authority over men in any shepherding oversight.

Paul gives two reasons for these spiritually principled injunctions. The first is that Adam was created first. Paul obviously sees this as God's way of establishing Adam, and subsequently males, in a position of authority and responsibility that He intended for him. This position of authority is crucial to God because it represents the principle of authority that finds its source in God Himself and is outlined in 1 Corinthians 11:3.

It also indicates that God highly values submission, in this context by women, to appropriately appointed authority in the affairs of mankind, especially including the Church. In an answer to the evangelical feminists, Schreiner asserts, "The proscription on women teaching men, then does not stem from the fall and cannot be ascribed to the curse. Paul appeals to the created order, the good and perfect world God has made, to justify the ban on women teaching men."

The second reason Paul gives for his prohibition of women in authority positions over men is that Eve was deceived, not Adam, which caused her to "[fall] into transgression" (1 Tim. 2:14). That Eve was deceived by Satan is stated by her in Genesis 3:13b where she confessed, "The serpent deceived me, and I ate."

In considering what this means, the deception implies that Eve thought she was doing the right thing, perhaps even improving on what God had instructed Adam about the tree of the knowledge of good and evil. Paul makes it clear in his instruction to Timothy that Adam was not deceived by Satan. He ate of the forbidden tree knowing that it was wrong to do so. Rather than being deceived by Satan, he was overwhelmed by his desire to please his wife.

God's first words of rebuke and correction to Adam were, "Because you have listened to the voice of your wife, and have eaten from the tree about which I commanded you, saying, 'You shall not eat from it'" (Genesis 3:17b). An important implication of these conversations is that authority and responsibility to lead are not given as rewards for good behavior, nor are they withheld due to bad behavior. Instead, God's message to Adam was this, and I paraphrase:

> You have not fulfilled your responsibility and place of authority to lead your wife in My ways for you. Instead you have, in your weakness and passivity in desiring to please your wife and allow her to lead you, disobeyed my clear and serious command concerning the tree.

To Eve, the message from God was this, and I again paraphrase:

> You took on a role of leadership I did not give you
> nor was it prepared for you when I made you. I
> did not intend for you to lead in the fight against
> evil in resisting Satan. Therefore, you fell into
> transgression because you took on a responsibility
> and role of leadership that I never intended for
> you.

This interpretation of God's communication to both Adam and Eve is the basis for Paul's prohibition of a woman teaching in an authoritative context or otherwise exercising authority over men. This explanation maintains integrity with the first reason for the prohibition, i.e. that of the priority of the creation order for Adam and Eve. It also does not falsely lead us to believe that Paul's prohibition of women is based on their failure to obey, since Adam's failure was even more pronounced.

Instead, it places the emphasis of the prohibition on the issue of God's order of authority where it belongs: His assignment of authority to the male members of humanity.

* * *

I now come to what most biblical commentators acknowledge to be one of the most troubling passages in the Scriptures—1 Timothy 2:15: "But women will be preserved through the bearing of children if they continue in faith and love and sanctity with self-restraint."

The word for "preserved" in the New American Standard Bible is the first future tense of *sodzo*. The root meaning of this word is "to save, to keep safe and sound, to rescue from danger or destruction," according to *Thayer's*. Its applied meanings include physical preservation and spiritual salvation.

The English Standard Version, the New Revised Standard Version, the New King James Version all translate this word as "saved." I assume that the translators of the NASB use the term "preserved" because they felt that physical preservation was the best way to think about this passage. The problem with this translation is that the context of the verse is more about spiritual salvation and living. The words "if they continue in faith and love and sanctity with self-restraint" all refer to the spiritual life of God's people, both men and women.

For a woman to be saved through childbearing cannot, for obvious reasons, mean she is saved (spiritually) by means of childbearing. The meaning could only be that she is saved through the process of childbearing. This interpretation can fit the spiritual salvation to which I believe this passage is referring. If so, then it would then mean that a woman is saved through the process of, not by means of, childbearing.

Pulling verses 14 and 15 together allows us to say that since Paul brought up the deception and transgression of Eve, it brought to his mind the curse that was placed on Eve and all women connected to childbearing. In other words, Paul didn't want his instruction to unduly discourage women as they are reminded of Eve's deception and transgression. As painful and miserable as is the process of childbearing, God's salvation is so wonderful that it overwhelms the fear and discouragement accompanying pregnancy and childbirth.

That process of pregnancy and childbearing will not keep any woman from fully receiving, enjoying, and living out the salvation she has in Jesus Christ. She will be saved in the midst of and passing through the process of childbearing, even though that process reminds her of the curse of deception and transgression that she shares with Eve.

The key to this interpretation all hinges on the preposition used in the Greek: *dia.* By way of disclaimer, I had five years of education in the Greek language and have used it throughout my life of preparing to teach from the New Testament. That said, I do not consider myself a Greek scholar by any means.

On the other hand, I'm able to read and, for the most part, understand the Greek lexical and exegetical works. I'm also aware of excellent scholars in this area who've added to my knowledge. One of them, A. T. Robertson, points out in his book, *A Grammar of the Greek New Testament in the Light of Historical Research,* that the root of *dia* is "two" and advances "a step further than merely 'two' to the idea of by-twain, be-tween, in two, and in twain."

Robertson then adds, "This is the ground-meaning in actual usage." After saying that this preposition is used usually with the genitive case, he moves to the sense of "passing between or through," a meaning that is present in many New Testament passages, including:

- Hebrews 11:29, which describes the Israelites as "passing through" the Red Sea.

- John 4:4, which says that Jesus "had to pass through Samaria."

- Romans 15:28, in which, in the NASB, Paul explains to the saints at Rome that he "will go on by way of you to Spain." The literal translation of the Greek is "I will go away through (*dia*) you to Spain."

Thayer's Greek-English Lexicon of the New Testament indicates rather clearly, with Robertson, that *dia* in the genitive case (like for the word "childbearing") can mean *through* in the sense of passing through. "Its tropical use of a state or condition in which one does or suffers something."

This fits exactly with what I interpret Paul to be saying. A woman, because of her connection to Eve's deception by Satan and falling into transgression, suffers the awareness of that failure as she experiences the physical suffering of childbearing. Her salvation through faith in Jesus Christ, however, will be fully experienced and will cause her to "pass through" that painful (both physical and spiritual) reminder with no loss of her relationship to her Savior and Lord if she is faithfully living out that relationship "in faith and love and sanctity with self-restraint," as Paul writes in 1 Timothy 2:15.

Fifteen to twenty years ago, Grace and I took one of our young grandchildren to Chuck E. Cheese's, which serves pizza inside a noisy indoor arcade. Even though many adults may enjoy this experience, all that stimulation was rather a nerve-wracking experience for us. We could say, nevertheless, that we survived (were saved) through (*dia*) that Chuck E. Cheese's experience.

It perhaps would be helpful to explain how this preposition, *dia*, is used in the accusative case. This usage of the word, mysteriously to me, is the way most biblical scholars and commentators have gone in the interpretation of this passage. In the accusative case, the word is used to designate "the means or instrument by which anything is affected," according to *Thayer's*. This forces commentators to say that a woman is saved "by means of" childbearing.

This is such an obviously impossible interpretation biblically that when this direction is taken, these commentators are forced into fanciful and forced explanations. I'm deeply thankful for the above scholarship (not mine!) that has given us a way to interpret this passage that honors the salvation message and the unique circumstance and blessing of womanhood.

Another thing this point of view does is give us a way to preserve the integrity and flow of the entire passage of 1 Timothy 2:9-15. Even though Paul has clearly limited women from positions of authority in the Church, he does not want to discourage them from the unique and powerful contributions they bring to their families and the Church. Bearing children is an extremely important issue to God and a major part of His assignment in ministry to women. Paul does not want the pain and stress of childbirth and its reminder of Eve's deception to make them feel like second-class servants of the living God because they most decidedly are not.

I realize I have taken a long time to deal with this qualification of gender for an elder, but I have done so because this issue is polarizing the church. The position of those who advocate for women elders is based, in my view of Scripture, on careless exegesis or intentional distorting of Scripture to fit the confused, wounded, and rebellious world culture in which we live.

I long for the unity of God's Church based on His clear ordering of our human sexuality in this present world of time and space. In heaven, our sexuality will no longer be an issue. That said, I'm convinced that clarity about authority and its blessing will be seen as an essential component of God's sovereign plan "with a view to an administration suitable to the fullness of the times," as Paul said in Ephesians 1:10a, "that is, the summing up of all things in Christ, things in the heavens and things on the earth."

Now I move into the selection process for elders and what that process should involve.

THE SELECTION PROCESS
FOR ELDERS

We now come to the important parts of the qualification process for an elder, which starts with a question: "How do you select elders in any given local congregation based on these qualifications?"

It's hard to overstate the importance of a substantial and effective answer to this pertinent question. Even for churches that are committed to the principle of authority being vested in qualified elders, this area of the selection process is where the principle can get cloudy or lost. The goal must be to develop—with God's help—the very best process to assure that the men selected as elders are God's choices as well.

In the church where I served as the senior pastor for many years, we developed a process that helped us know we had done our best to hear from God regarding His choice of men to be our elders. I'm certain this process can be improved upon, and our best efforts over the years did not guarantee absolutely perfect results.

Nonetheless, with some adaptation and improvement, this process is a great place to start as a basis for our understanding of how this can work.

There are several presuppositions that are important to acknowledge in the elder selection process. First of all, I don't find it inconsistent with the principle of the "priesthood of all believers" nor the equal value of each member of the Body of Christ to acknowledge that certain individuals have gifts that equip them to function as elders and certain individuals do not.

Nor is it inconsistent to acknowledge that certain individuals are of greater spiritual maturity than others, which would allow them to function as elders. Nor is it inconsistent to acknowledge that, while it's difficult and not always unquestionably clear, the present elders of the church—along with the affirmation of the congregation—need to discern the qualifications and readiness of certain individuals to be elders.

Secondly, an important point to keep in mind is that elders should be perceived as lay pastors. This means that their role and responsibility encompass more than leading a Bible study discussion, conducting prayer time, chairing a church meeting, or engaging in any number of other church-related activities. The essence of shepherding/pastoring is taking primary human responsibility—in conjunction with the Lord—for the spiritual welfare of other individuals.

In 1 Peter 5:3, the apostle Peter, in speaking to the elders of the churches, refers to "those allotted to your charge." This "charge" refers to the command to "shepherd the flock of God among you" (verse 2). This is the responsibility of each elder on the elder team.

Thirdly, as far as I've been able to discern, errors in the selection process of elders have always been on the side of premature appointment. Therefore, including the clear cautions of the Training Network of the Evangelical Free Church (a training process provided by our denomination for our core leadership), it's imperative to be as carefully responsible as you can in the appointment of elders.

Here's a comprehensive list of prerequisites that need to be observed by elders, other church leaders, and the congregation before the selection process begins:

1. A minimum of two years' involvement in an accountability small group to ensure that this candidate is

intimately known by a responsible segment of the congregation.

2. A minimum of one year in some leadership capacity that involves shepherding other believers. It should be clear to existing leadership that he knows how to relate to people and lead them in God's Word and ways.

3. A substantial demonstration that the individual is committed to the basic disciplines of Bible study, prayer, fellowship, and evangelism.

4. A substantial demonstration that the individual understands and is committed to the philosophy of ministry and core values of the local church in which he fellowships and serves.

5. A substantial commitment to preserving the unity of the Spirit in the bond of peace within the church.

6. A substantial commitment to the biblical principle of male headship in the home and in the church in a healthy and godly way.

7. A substantial commitment to the whole body of his local church and demonstration of a balanced, consistent participation in the worship service (celebration), a fellowship/ministry group (congregation), and an accountability small group (cell).

In addition to these qualifications, there are a few practical issues to mention. A key one is that an elder candidate should be teachable and be willing to serve joyfully under authority. This is crucial because being teachable with a good attitude paves the way for an individual to be strengthened in the areas where he is weak.

The elder candidate needs to be spiritually, emotionally, and psychologically healthy, and he must not be so burdened with his needs that he is unable to bear the stress and burdens of others. A candidate should be secure enough in his relationship to God that he is at peace with himself and not overly dependent upon others or fearfully withdrawn from others.

With those introductory thoughts, here's how I see the elder selection process beginning:

1. The individual is observed by a small group leader, pastoral staff, other small group participants, ministry team leaders, and elders over a period of one to two years to see if he manifests the above prerequisites and qualifications.

2. As the observers become aware of his emerging gifts and growing spiritual maturity, they share their thoughts and impressions about the individual with each other and begin asking if the individual is ready to be considered for eldership. This communication can take place in elder meetings, other leadership gatherings, or informally among the various leaders as they stay in contact with one another.

3. As the answers to the above questions become increasingly positive, the elders acknowledge that the individual is a potential elder candidate.

4. The elders then contact the individual and ask him if he would be willing to be nominated as a potential elder and go through a process that would allow the elders and congregation as well as him to hear from God about his being appointed as an elder.

5. If the individual is willing and is aware that God is leading him to be part of the process, he is invited to spend an extensive amount of time with the elders and other male leadership in the church. There will be an interview based on the elder qualifications document prepared from 1 Timothy 3 and Titus 1. The individual will be encouraged to speak as openly and honestly as he can about his strengths and weaknesses in relationship to these biblical qualifications. The men gathered then share their assessment of the individual's strengths and weaknesses. If there is consensus to move ahead, a recommendation is made to the elders who then, at a separate meeting, decide to continue the process.

6. The individual then meets with the elders along with his wife and goes through the same review process based on the biblical qualifications. If he has teenage children or older, the elders will meet with them at a separate time without the parents.

7. The individual then meets with elders and the members of his accountability small group (if that structure is available), or a small group of individuals who know him best in the church. They go through the same review process.

8. The elders then meet with the women of his wife's accountability small group or the equivalent without him or her for the same review process.

9. If there is no significant obstacle to his appointment as an elder, a letter is sent from the elders to an unbelieving employer, colleague, neighbor, or family member, asking that person to write a letter of

reference concerning their view of this man and his qualifications to be a leader in the church.

10. If everything is substantially positive to this point, a letter is sent to the congregation stating that the elders are ready to appoint this man to full elder- ship, asking for any input they might have. Their response is to be in writing, signed by the person, or delivered in person to one of the existing elders. A period of thirty days will be allowed for this process to be completed.

11. If there is no significant negative input, the elders can appoint the individual as an elder for confirma- tion by the congregation.

12. This appointment is communicated to the entire voting membership of the congregation for their con- firmation vote of yes or no. This can be done by mail or by a specially called meeting or at the regularly scheduled annual meeting. The confirmation must be by a 75 percent positive vote, at which time the man officially becomes an elder.

I submit this thorough process gives God the opportunity to let us know—through our leadership and His people—what His mind is about this individual. Having used this process for several decades, I've found that it has substantially helped God's people to feel secure in His appointment of their leaders.

How are elders supposed to function in their leadership role? I'll share some thoughts in my next-to-last chapter.

18

THE PRACTICAL FUNCTION OF ELDERS

How should biblically qualified elders function in their leadership role in the local church?

In this important chapter, I will summarize the main functions and responsibilities for elders.

The Function of Shepherding the Flock

I see an elder's main responsibility as being one who can "shepherd the church of God" (Acts 20:28-30; 1 Peter 5:1-2).

This means being part of a comprehensive ministry of caring for the spiritual and physical needs of every member of the flock. This responsibility is spoken of reverently and rather intimidatingly (for the elders) in Hebrews 13:17 as "[keeping] watch over [their] souls." Peter adds that it involves "exercising oversight" (1 Peter 5:2) and makes it clear that this leadership is not one of control or in any way oppressive but is based on modelling a healthy and mature spiritual life before the people (1 Peter 5:3).

Paul, in his passionate and moving exhortation to the Ephesian elders in Acts 20, indicates that they have the awesome responsibility of protecting the flock from false teaching and division among the people (Acts 20:28-31). Based on Jesus' commission to Peter in John 21:15-17, the apostles and elders are to "tend [the] lambs," "shepherd [the] sheep," and "tend [the] sheep."

One of the major responsibilities in shepherding is feeding the sheep. In the Church, this involves the high gifting and exhortation to teach the people God's Word. This is a major part of Christ's great commission to the apostles to "[teach] them to observe all that I commanded you" (Matthew 28:18-20).

This responsibility is echoed for elders in Titus 1:9 where their qualifications include "holding fast the faithful word which is in accordance with the teaching, so that he will be able both to exhort in sound doctrine and to refute those who contradict." This is repeated in Paul's solemn exhortation to Timothy, whom he appointed as the provisional elder/leader in Ephesus in 2 Timothy 4:1-2:

> I solemnly charge you in the presence of God and
> of Christ Jesus, who is to judge the living and the
> dead, and by His appearing and His kingdom:
> preach the word; be ready in season and out
> of season; reprove, rebuke, exhort, with great
> patience and instruction.

As important as the teaching role is for elders, another equally important role is "equipping of the saints for the work of service, to the building up of the body of Christ" (Ephesians 4:12b). This equipping is quite comprehensive and includes doing whatever is necessary to prepare men and women—the "saints" in the Church—to fulfill their calling before God as serving members of the Body of Christ. This equipping is to take into account the gifts given to each individual member by the Holy Spirit (1 Corinthians 12). This is the process and pattern for healthy, effective, and godly church growth. The ministry of elders is aimed directly at God's people becoming mature, loving, Christlike members of the Body of Christ (Ephesians 4:11-16).

Elders Functioning in a Plurality

How does a team of elders function with authority as a team in relationship to one another?

One of the most ignored principles of authority in the Church is that of plurality. In Scripture, references to an elder's function are always plural (e.g. Acts 14:23; Titus 1:5; Acts 20:17-30; and 1 Peter 5:1-4). More often than not, the senior or lead pastor either takes the authority or it's given to him by the other church leaders.

Sometimes the authority is—for a lack of a better word—confiscated by one of the elders who is either stronger in leadership, gifting, and personality or contributes a large amount of money to the church, or all of the above. This is extremely dangerous for the church and for the man himself.

Authority should never be vested in one man. He doesn't have enough gifts for a balanced leadership and ministry. He will have insufficient accountability in dealing with his "blind spots" and failures. He will have incomplete support in the stresses and struggles of pastoral ministry. And this much power has a high potential of destroying him and the church—I've seen it happen too often.

The authority of Jesus through the elders is not focused on individual elders in the New Testament. Rather, it's clearly focused on the united plurality of them in the presence of God to hear His word and to be led by His Spirit for the building of His church.

In the crucial discussions about truth, policies, methodologies, focus, and scope of ministry, etc., each elder is indwelt and gifted uniquely by God's Spirit. Each man needs to be empowered and encouraged to speak with the others about what God is saying to him. No one elder, including the senior or lead pastor, should advocate his position but rather submit his position to the process of discussion with the entire eldership before God and His Word and in prayer, listening to His Spirit.

One of the most exciting experiences among the elders is

anticipating God's leading through all of them, blending their thoughts and concerns into a united decision by the Holy Spirit for the good of the Church and for the glory of God. With that said, I have listened to pastors express how much they dislike their board meetings over the years. One friend of mine who was hired as a part-time pastor after his retirement related to me that he told the church leaders he would be glad to serve if he never had to go to another board meeting.

It shouldn't be that way. I have to confess that once we established a biblically qualified eldership in our church, I looked forward to our elder meetings as much if not more than any other aspect of the ministry. It was not that we were all perfect or spiritually superior, but we all knew we were hearing from God together about His church, which was the greatest privilege we could experience as we shepherded "His flock."

I must add, however, that this only took place after we submitted ourselves to His Word and His Spirit and to each other to hear what He would say to us from each of us.

The Relationship of a Senior Pastor with the Elders

A corollary issue to this principle of plurality is how it actually works in the relationship between the senior or lead pastor and the eldership team in terms of authority and how that's applied to the overall ministry of the church.

I'm convinced that this relationship can be experienced with great unity and joy if the senior pastor understands and is committed to the principle of authority in the church based on the teaching of God's Word concerning elders. A senior pastor should absolutely avoid with everything in him ever referring to this ministry as "my church." The Church belongs to Jesus alone. He has delegated His authority through the apostles to the elders to be the "under-shepherds" of the Church.

The senior pastor needs to view himself as one of the elders and submit himself to them in their plurality, just as each of them should also do with him. He also needs to understand that one of his highest priorities should be to "empower" the eldership by developing them, training them, trusting them, and willingly submitting to them. This is how God protects the Church from him and him from the Church.

In this manner, those in leadership will know together that they are leading and shepherding this flock of God in His ways. It will also be helpful and necessary for him and the elders to acknowledge that there is a natural and healthy tension between how he submits to their authority and how much freedom the elders give him to exercise authority and leadership in day-to-day ministry.

This balance is crucial and requires the leading of God's Spirit in the senior pastor and the elders. In a sense, because the lead pastor is clearly gifted, adequately trained, and given time through his hired position, he is the "first among equals." This is why the lead pastor must give high priority to empowering the eldership to function in its plurality. This is a delicate balance that only God's Spirit can provide.

Elders Must Function Supernaturally

Another consideration of how the elder team is to function together in leading God's people has to do with the spiritual, supernatural component of the process. The leadership of the eldership is not to be based on human opinion, preference, or experience. Instead, the leadership is to be based on how God's Holy Spirit blends everything that each elder brings to the table with the other elders and infuses this leadership group with His discernment, wisdom, power, and love.

Each meeting together should be characterized by the supernatural presence of God through His Spirit. How this takes place is modeled for us through the apostles in Acts 6. When the physical, material needs of the "Hellenistic" widows were being neglected, the apostles—knowing this was an important issue—responded with these words: "It is not desirable for us to neglect the word of God in order to serve tables" (Acts 6:2b). Because they knew this ministry was important, they told the congregation to select some men, "full of the Spirit and of wisdom, whom we may put in charge of this task" (verse 3b).

This is a great example of how the apostles, in the position of authority, worked with the congregation to select these first "deacons" to carry out an important ministry. After the congregation did its work at the direction of the apostles, they brought the seven men back to the apostles for their approval and commissioning with prayer and the laying on of their hands.

The apostles, in delegating this task to the deacons, explained, "But we will devote ourselves to prayer and to the ministry of the word" (verse 4). These two areas of focus indicate how the apostles, and later elders, assured that their ministry of authority and leadership would be the faithful representation of Jesus as the Head of the Church caring for His flock.

The ministry of God's Word is the way elders hold "fast the faithful word which is in accordance with the teaching, so that [they] will be able both to exhort in sound doctrine and to refute those who contradict" (Titus 1:9). Without the Word of God central in every deliberation and decision, the Church is in the hands of human thinking, experiences, preferences, and wisdom. The Word of God must be central so the elders can discern the supernatural issues and directives necessary to lead the Church in God's ways, not man's.

The ministry of prayer is the way that the apostles could discern the leading of God's Spirit in the specific application of the truth and principles of God's Word to any current issue or ministry. Prayer is the way we listen to God's Spirit and yield to His control. This is dramatically exampled for us in the first two chapters of the Book of Acts. Jesus had told the eleven apostles not to begin any ministry but to wait for the promise of the Father to send His Spirit to empower them and lead them. They spent ten days fellowshipping and praying in the upper room until the day of Pentecost arrived.

Prayer prepared them and their small congregation for the powerful work of God's Spirit in the sound of a rushing, mighty wind, cloven tongues of fire on the heads of each person, and the supernatural expression of praise and worship in the languages of all the people who had come from the Mediterranean world to worship in Jerusalem on the feast of Pentecost.

Here is the pattern for elders in the ministry of the Word and prayer. This is the way they hear from God through His Spirit on behalf of Jesus, the Head of the church. This resulted in the first sermon, preached by Peter, about the life, ministry, death, and resurrection of Jesus. The power of God's Spirit through Peter's message effected the supernatural repentance and baptism of three thousand souls that day.

For elders to lead God's people in God's ways, they must immerse themselves and their ministry in the ministry of the Word and prayer. Their role is to listen to God through His Spirit. This is the indispensable factor in every gathering of the elder team.

When I first began a ministry at the church where I served for forty-two years, the meetings of the administrative board (the main authority structure in a confused authority system) did not come close to what I have just described for an elder team. I cannot remember anyone ever referring to Scripture in our deliberations. Prayer was brief before the meeting. The men and women on the board were for the most part believers, but for the most part as well, they were not biblically qualified to be in a place of authority.

The difference between those experiences and what I enjoyed for the last twenty to twenty-five years of being part of an elder team that followed the "power of submission" principles that I've shared in this book was night and day. I honestly looked forward to every time our elder team gathered. This was not because we were without human flaws and limitations. The reason I looked forward in expectation was because I knew we were coming together to listen to God alone and none of us was committed to our own agenda, opinions, or preferences. Instead, we were committed to submitting ourselves to God's Spirit and to one another.

That's why I covet a biblically qualified elder team listening to God on behalf of every local church that wants to honor Jesus Christ as the only Head of His church.

The Elders and the Congregation

A final and critical concern about the practical function of the elder team regards their relationship to the congregation. Since the submission of the congregation is a willing submission on their part rather than coercive, the elders need to be constantly aware of building a relationship of trust with them. There are several ways to effect this kind of trust.

First, the entire elder selection process should be made known to the congregation. When that happens, the congregation will have a sense that the elders are doing their very best to listen to God about the selection of the men to be elders. The congregation's 75 percent affirmation (or greater) of the elder appointees, which is required in the selection process, reminds everyone that the elders respected their input and wanted them to have an integral part in the process.

Second, prior to the time of the congregation's annual meeting to approve the budget, affirm the new elders (the existing elders were also affirmed annually by at least 75 percent margin), or deal with any other major issues, the elders should hold a congregational forum.

During this time, various issues and topics can be presented and questions or comments can be encouraged and received. The congregational forum is not a time of voting but a time for the elders to receive input and ask the people to pray with them and for them in their decision process. The people will understand that the elders are listening respectfully and that they are to pray for God's leading among them, which is affirmed by a yes or no vote from the congregation at the annual meeting.

Third, when there is an issue in which the elders want input, they should appoint several people from the congregation with some training, experience, and expertise to become part of an "advisory team" to the elders. These qualified people should be known by the elders to be spiritually mature followers of Jesus who only want His way for the church, not their own. They should be willing to share their opinions and suggestions without demanding their way and should also know that they are not an authority structure but an important "advisory" structure to help the elders in their decision-making process.

Finally, the elders should establish what is known as an "Equippers Community." This is made up of key leaders of the church, both men and women. They can be small group leaders, deacons, other major ministry leaders, and pastoral ministry staff. They should meet monthly with the elders for training, unity building, information, input to the elders about current issues, and prayer. They should become an extension of the elders to receive input from the congregation to the elders and give direction and information from the elders to the congregation.

The Equippers Community is not a decision-making structure, which is reserved for the elders. The formation of this group is a good way to involve more of the congregation with the elder team.

One thing is true about all systems developed by humans: they are flawed. Having said that, these four ways of listening to and engaging the congregation can be very effective in building trust between the elders and the people, for which I give great praise and thanksgiving to God.

In summation, my prayer for every Bible-believing church is that they will make a commitment to these powerful and freeing principles of authority in their local church. If they do, they will experience—by God's Spirit—the power of submission.

19

SOME FINAL THOUGHTS

Authority and Submission in Creation

As I come to a close, I want to spend some time reflecting on how the subject of authority is a major principle that God has built into all of created life.

First of all, this principle of authority is seen in the vast expanse of the universe. God's Word says this in Isaiah 40:26:

> Lift up your eyes on high
> And see who has created these stars,
> The One who leads forth their host by number,
> He calls them all by name;
> Because of the greatness of His might and the
> strength of His power,
> Not one of them is missing.

The awesome, powerful seas of the world bow in submission to the boundaries with "a bolt and doors" placed upon them by God, as His Word says in Job 38:10, which continues in verse 11b when He says:

> Thus far you shall come, but no farther;
> And here shall your proud waves stop.

The fact that nature obeys a universal "order" that comes from God was enough to change the mind of Antony Flew, a world-renowned philosopher who was arguably the best-known atheist in the English-speaking world throughout much of the latter half of the 20th century. Flew accepted the existence of God in 2004 and stated at that time that "the most impressive arguments for God's existence are those that are supported by recent scientific discoveries" and that "the argument to Intelligent Design is enormously stronger than it was when I first met it." It should be an encouragement to all of us to see that the laws of nature coming from God are not a mere hypothesis or theory but actually an established principle of His that works.

To further explain myself, I want to begin in a rather strange place and ask you to consider how this principle works in the relationship between a human and his or her dog.

Perhaps you've heard of Cesar Millan, who's known as the "Dog Whisperer" on the National Geographic Wild cable channel. Over many years of observing and working with all sorts of breeds of dogs and their different personalities, Cesar has distilled his findings on how to train a dog to be a happy, healthy, and a psychologically stable pet and companion in his book, *Cesar's Way*.

"The concept of a 'pack' is ingrained in your dog's DNA," Cesar writes. "In a pack, there are only two roles: the role of leader and the role of follower. If you don't become your dog's pack leader, he will assume that role and try to dominate you."

Cesar says that your role as the dog owner and pack leader is to be "calmly assertive" with the goal of training your dog to be "calmly submissive." The application of these principles concerning authority will produce "miraculous" results in the lives of dogs and their owners. What's so fascinating about these principles is their amazing effect on the other areas of community life. Cesar then writes this:

> After applying my techniques, you may even
> begin to understand yourself better. You'll look
> at your own behavior in a different light and may
> find yourself changing the ways you interact with
> your children, your spouse, or your boss. After
> all, humans are pack animals too! I've heard from
> more viewers than you might imagine that my

techniques have helped as many humans as they have dogs.

He then includes an astonishing letter from a viewer of his show, who wrote this:

Dear Cesar,

Thank you so much for your show *Dog Whisperer*. The funny thing is you've changed me and my family's life and we don't even own a dog. I am a forty-one-year-old mother of two (a five-year-old son and a six-year-old daughter). I was having a terrible time disciplining them (I learned they had no boundaries and limitations). My kids were pushing me around, literally, in public places and at home. And then I saw your show.

Since then I have trained myself to become a more assertive parent, using a more authority energy, demanding my space as an authority figure. I have also trained myself not to ask and beg them to do things, but to tell them to do things (such as clean up their room, clean their eating area, and put away their laundered clothes). My life has changed and so have they. To my amazement, my children have become more disciplined (and there's less fighting), and I found they actually like responsibilities and chores. They are proud when they accomplish a given task, and I am just thrilled.

You have not only taught humans about their dogs, you have taught humans about themselves.

Thank you so much!

The Capino Family

You may ask why these principles of authority work so power-fully. Remember the title of this book—*The Power of Submission*? These principles are ordained by God through His Word and infused into all areas of created existence. These are part of the "laws of nature" Antony Flew refers to. When followed, they work. In addition, when followed, God supports you in your obedience to His ways.

This is the power of submission.

Authority and Submission in an Oppressive Culture

The actual idea for my book title came to me from an unex-pected source—a Hollywood movie.

One of my Top Ten favorite movies is *Driving Miss Daisy*, which is a story about an aging Southern lady by the name of Miss Daisy. Played by Jessica Tandy, she is a fiercely indepen-dent and somewhat obnoxiously proud and willful woman used to getting her own way.

Overlaying her personal character is the oppressive, racist culture of the South in the 1940s regarding people of color as well as Jews, which Miss Daisy was. Entering the story at this point is a black chauffeur hired by Miss Daisy's son to drive her around town to appointments and errands. The chauffeur, named Hoke, is masterfully played by Morgan Freeman. He's a confident, competent, and kind African-American man determined to carry out his assigned role as a driver for Miss Daisy.

His biggest problem is that Miss Daisy does not want to be driven by anybody. She has had her own car for decades, which allowed her to come and go at her pleasure. With old age, however, her driving skills had deteriorated to the point where she had become a danger to herself and others when behind the wheel of a car.

One of the more humorous scenes in the movie is watching Miss Daisy walk to town rather than submit to the indignity of being driven by Hoke. As she strides along the sidewalk, we are privileged to see Hoke driving the car alongside her all the way into town at the same pace she is walking. This creative submission to the one he is serving does not keep Hoke from relentlessly and kindly carrying out the assignment for which he was hired. Instead, this relentless sense of responsibility establishes Hoke as the strongest character in the movie. His kindness and continuous sense of responsibility is applied in amazingly creative ways and dominates the narrative of this unlikely relationship between him and Miss Daisy.

Over a period of time, their relationship grows as Hoke patiently continues to serve Miss Daisy. She softens her personality and slowly accepts having a hired chauffeur. They share many adventures and trips together that become increasingly warm and friendly.

After a period of time goes by, Miss Daisy is plagued with dementia. One morning, when Hoke comes to check on her, she is agitated and panicked about her teaching lessons for the day. Since she has not taught school for many years, Hoke seeks to quiet her and remind her that she is no longer a teacher.

After some strong but loving words from Hoke, she quiets down and sits in a chair as Hoke continues to stay near her. She takes his hand and looking up into his face, she says, "Hoke, you are my best friend."

She is later seen living in an assisted living retirement home when Hoke comes to visit her. The movie's climax, at least for me, came when Hoke, who is also aging, arrives at lunch time and sits with her at her table. When she has difficulty controlling her shaking hands, Hoke takes her fork and gently feeds her pumpkin pie, one bite at a time, which she quietly and thankfully receives.

The movie ends, and we are left to reflect on the powerful message of this story. For me, the meaning is clear. Hoke found a way to transcend both the racist culture in which he lived and the self-centered character of Miss Daisy by submitting to the unjust and unrighteous nature of both. This sets him free to not only serve Miss Daisy but to also express kindness, care, and love as he carries out the mundane duty of being her chauffeur.

I was greatly moved at this expression of respect and contentment by Hoke under the authority of an oppressive culture and a selfish, willful woman, who grew in kindness and love because of his actions.

This is the power of submission.

Authority and Submission in the Mission Field

The power of obeying God's Word on the path of submission to God-ordained authority is movingly displayed in the story of Joanne Shetler, a Wycliffe Bible translator. She has written a thrilling account of her twenty-plus years among the Balangao people of the Philippines in her book, *And the Word Came with Power.*

Her mission to translate the New Testament into the Balangao language involved her and her Balangao helpers in the New Testament Scriptures. As a result, a thriving Balangao church was planted in addition to providing them the New Testament in their own language.

If you choose to read *And the Word Came with Power*, you will find yourself giving thanks and praise to God for His faithfulness to His powerful Word that "breaks the power of cancelled sin, [that] sets the prisoner free," as the old hymn, *O for a Thousand Tongues to Sing*, says. You will also thank God for the faithfulness of this godly and faith-driven single woman who's served these people through His Word and through His Spirit.

One of the things that impacted me in her book was the way Joanne tapped in to this principle of submission to God-appointed authority in her life. When she and her translation partner, Anne, arrived in the village of Botac in the Balangao valley, they were aware that this would be their home for an extended period of time. They spent the first night in a "huge" home (14 feet by 16 feet, or 224 square feet) provided for them by Canao, the spokesman of the village. He fed them dinner which, by Balangao cultural standards, became a "pledge to protect that person with his own life."

After a few days of Joanne and Anne setting up housekeeping, Canao:

> . . . walked in looking quite serious, without a trace of his usual smile. He was outwardly calm, but we could feel his tension and heard it in his voice. "Don't you realize it's not safe for women to be here? Don't you know we're headhunters?"
>
> He let that sink in and then, with a sigh, said, "You need someone to take care of you—I'll be your father!" He gave a short, deliberate nod, sealing his words with final authority.

Joanne and Anne's response to Canao is fascinating:

> We looked across the room at that wiry little man, barefoot and wearing tattered short pants. At five-foot-two, he probably didn't weigh much over one hundred pounds. Some missing front teeth made him lisp; we couldn't understand him very well. The few teeth he had were stained red from chewing betel nut. We knew he'd never even been to high school. He seemed a little pushy. He

was always telling us what to do. He had already made up a list of words that he thought we needed to learn and had tested us on them.

Both Joanne and Anne were thinking that "people don't have substitute fathers." They compromised and told him they would call him uncle. Joanne's narrative at this point is very telling. She writes, "But Mariano Canao Lucasi was a perceptive man. He knew what we were thinking. And he was a wise man—he ignored it."

Canao not only took personal responsibility for Joanne and Anne, but he also mobilized "everyone" to help take care of them. At a peace pact ceremony where the men sang and chanted, Canao "broke into song; he chanted that we were his daughters and we ate in his house. He was announcing that all the rules that guarded Balangaos were guarding us."

"Uncle" Canao watched over Joanne and Anne, helping them to relate wisely to the Balangao culture. At first they questioned his advice, but "soon Uncle Canao proved himself to us, and whatever he suggested, we did."

As they began to progress in learning the Balangao language, Joanne and Anne began calling Canao "Ama"—Father. "And saying it in Balangao sounded right. Uncle Canao became Ama," Joanne wrote.

Her reflection on this process is striking:

> In those days, we had just a glimmer of under-standing about God's gift to us through Ama. We didn't comprehend that our new family was Mark 10:29 coming true for us. God was giving back to us what we'd left for His sake.

When Anne, with Joanne's blessing and God's leading, left the mission field and got married, Ama told Joanne that from now on she must eat all her meals with his family. His reason: *So you won't get lonely*. This relationship with Ama and his family were one of the main reasons the Wycliffe administration allowed Joanne to continue her work without another partner.

After Anne left, Joanne depended more on her Balangao family for help, advice, and companionship. She also related how one night some men brought a drunk Ama home and dumped him on the floor. Joanne hated it whenever Ama got drunk because it embarrassed her. This time, as she left his house in frustration, she spoke out loud:

> Now what am I going to do? You're my father, and you're supposed to advise me. But when you're drunk, I don't have anyone to go to—what am I going to do?

He must have heard enough of what she said because Joanne writes, "He never drank again."

Perhaps unknowingly, by speaking truth, Joanne had discovered how to empower Ama as her Balangao father to lead, care for, and protect her with the authority God had provided for her in him. This leadership on the part of Ama, and Joanne's willing and wise submission to him, manifested itself in an important way in the planting of a thriving church.

When Joanne had finished the translation of 1 John, she gave it to Ama to correct the grammar because she had taught him to read Balangao. As he went over 1 John in his own language, he became very excited about the truth of God he was reading. "My child," he said, "these words are good! People would believe this if they could just hear it."

The next Sunday, Ama and a sizeable group of people, without telling Joanne ahead of time, showed up at her "huge" house. "Here we are, teach us," they said. This group grew to about sixty people. While some people believed in Jesus right away during the teaching time, Joanne was burdened and frustrated with the significant resistance from the "spirits" who hounded the rest until they sacrificed to them. The spirits attacked the people physically with sickness and fear. Joanne also felt "increasingly uncomfortable being their only teacher," she said.

Joanne asked the people to start teaching, but they refused. "We don't know enough to teach," they said. Then one day, while she and Ama were checking over their translation of 1 Timothy, they came to the second chapter where Paul writes, "I do not permit a woman to teach . . . a man" (1 Tim. 2:12b).

Without saying anything to Joanne, the next Sunday Ama got up before the people and said, "My daughter here knows more about this than I do, but we found in the Bible where it says that women aren't supposed to teach men, so I guess I have to be the one." Joanne wrote, "My Balangao teaching career was over. Ama led the Balangaos into church leadership."

There were abundant ways that God accomplished His purpose of bringing the gospel through the Word of God that was translated into the Balangao language by Joanne Shetler. My purpose in referring to her and her book is to highlight the importance of God's principle of authority in the planting of His church among the Balangao people.

Joanne, knowingly or unknowingly, honored this principle in accepting the authority of Ama in her life as her "father" and later as the leader/elder of the Balangao church. It is my conviction that her obedience to God's Word concerning this principle of authority in her ministry and her relationship to the Balangao people released the power of God's Spirit to do an amazing work among them in the planting of a thriving church.

This is the power of submission.

My Personal Testimony Concerning
Authority and Submission

When I first began ministering at the church where I served for forty-two years with a congregational governance structure, the meetings of the Administrative Board (the main authority structure in a confused authority system) did not come close to what I have described as a biblically qualified elder team.

I cannot remember anyone ever referring to Scripture in our deliberations. Prayer was brief at the beginning of each meeting. The men and women on the board were for the most part believers, but they were also for the most part not biblically qualified to be in a place of authority.

During my time as pastor in this church, based on my preaching through major books of the New Testament and extensive prayer and conversation with the existing leadership, we incrementally moved from being a congregation-led church to being an elder-led church. Even though the process was not easy, that major transformation became a freedom for me and a basis for unity among our elders and in our congregation.

The difference between those experiences and what I enjoyed for the last twenty to twenty-five years at this same church, while being part of our elder team, was night and day. I honestly looked forward to every time our elder team gathered. This was not because we were without human flaws and limitations. It was, as previously indicated, because I knew we were coming together to listen to God alone and not one of us was committed to our own agenda, opinions, or preferences. We were committed to submitting ourselves to God's Spirit and to one another.

Over those years, I have done much teaching concerning eldership, which became a source of ministry after I retired. During this time, I've had the privilege of establishing biblically qualified elders as the basis of authority in various churches throughout Southern California. In each instance, under God's Spirit, this quickly became a source of healing, love, and unity in those churches after years of turmoil.

The reason I have written *The Power of Submission* is not because I am looking for financial reward. Nor have I had any ambition to become a published author. Instead, I've labored on this book because I have a passion for God's people, the Church.

I desire with all that is in me that pastors, elders, seminary professors, seminary students, and congregations have a clear understanding of God's authority in the world, the family, and the Church based on the clear teaching of the Scriptures. The lack of clarity on this subject has brought division and disunity to personal relationships, families, employees, employers, churches, parachurch organizations, and governments. The resistance and hatred of authority is rampant in our society and is multiplying exponentially, bringing chaos and strife everywhere.

On the other hand, I have experienced the opposite when God's people submit to His authority through the human agencies under which He has placed them. The result of this obedience to God's ways results in a love and unity that brings blessing and peace to everyone.

And that's the power of submission.

SOURCE MATERIAL

Introduction

"Barry Cooper, an English author, speaker, and church planter . . ." is from his article "Are You Worshipping the Idol of 'Open Options/?" in *Christianity Today*, January/February 2013 issue.

"Perhaps an answer to my question can be found in a column by John Leo that appeared in *U.S. News & World Report . . .*" is from the October 24, 1999 issue.

"The situation thus called for a boldness which Freud supplied . . ." is from *Freud and the Jewish Mystical Tradition,* by David Balkan, pages 114 and 117.

"Consider what Miley Cyrus, a Disney performer in her earlier years . . ." is from a *Yahoo News* story from August 29, 2015.

Chapter 1: God as the Source of All Authority

"That an earthly king should have his sovereignty acknowledged in this way . . ." is from *Barnes' Notes on Isaiah*, Vol. III, page 17.

"Paul places the whole question on a very high plane . . ." is from *The Epistle of Paul to the Romans by F.F. Bruce,* Intervarsity Press, 1963, page 233.

"This is a very comprehensive proposition . . ." is from Charles Hodge, *Commentary on the Epistle to the Romans,* Wm. B. Erdmans Publishing Company, 1955, page 406.

"People became slaves in various ways . . ." is from Edwin A. Blum, "1 Peter" in *The Expositor's Bible Commentary*, Zondervan, 1981, Vol. 12, page 225.

Chapter 2: The Hatred of Authority by Satan and Humans

"Grudem then relates how in Genesis 3 . . .' " is from *Systematic Theology: An Introduction to Biblical Doctrine* by Wayne Grudem, Zondervan, 2009, page 412.

"The initial *Why* sets the tone of its approach . . ." is from *Psalms 1-72* by Derek Kidner, Intervarsity Press, 1973, page 50.

Chapter 3: Authority and Submission Modeled in the Godhead

"For any earthly king, this form of address . . ." is from *Psalms 1-72* by Derek Kidner, Intervarsity Press, 1973, page 51.

"The absence of the article . . ." is from *The Epistle to the Hebrews* by Brook Foss Westcott, Macmillan and Co., 1920, page 7.

"*In Son* has reference . . ." is from *An Exposition of Hebrews*, by Arthur Pink, Prisbrary Publishing, 2012, Vol. I, page 26.

"So we may say that the role of the Father in creation . . ." is from *Systematic Theology: An Introduction to Biblical Doctrine* by Wayne Grudem, Zondervan, 2009, page 249.

"The Father would have ceased to be the Father . . ." is from *Systematic Theology: An Introduction to Biblical Doctrine* by Wayne Grudem, Zondervan, 2009, page 249.

". . . the Son of God is, in this his essential majesty. . ." is from *The Greek Testament* by Henry Alford, Waterloo Place; and Deighton, Bell, and Co., Cambridge, 1859, Vol. IV, page 7.

"The truth about the Trinity has sometimes . . ." is from *Systematic Theology: An Introduction to Biblical Doctrine* by Wayne Grudem, Zondervan, 2009, page 251.

"It was necessary that Christ's consent . . ." is from *An Exposition of Hebrews*, by Arthur Pink, Prisbrary Publishing, 2012, Vol. 2, pages 53-54.

"Perhaps the most dangerous symptom in popular theology. . ." is from *The Epistle to the Hebrews* by Brook Foss Westcott, Macmillan and Co., 1920, page 59.

"He Who is the Father of men is also the source . . ." is from *The Epistle to the Hebrews* by Brook Foss Westcott, Macmillan and Co., 1920, page 50.

"That principle is, that order . . ." is from Charles Hodge, *Commentary on the Epistle to the Romans,* Grand Rapids: Wm. B. Erdmans Publishing Company, 1955, p. 206.

"That principle is, that order and subordination. . ." is from Charles Hodge, *Commentary on the Epistle to the Romans,* Wm. B. Erdmans Publishing Company, 1955, p. 336.

Chapter 5: Godly Authority as It Applies to the Home

"That principle is, that order and subordination. . ." is from Charles Hodge, *Commentary on the Epistle to the Romans,* Wm. B. Erdmans Publishing Company, 1955, page 206.

"Paul emphasizes that man was created . . ." is by Douglas Moo in *Recovering Biblical Manhood & Womanhood*, John Piper and Wayne Grudem, editors, Crossway Books, 1991, page 190.

"Paul's appeal to the prior formation . . ." is from *Man and Woman In Biblical Perspective*, by James Hurley, Wipf & Stock Publishing, 2002, page 207.

Chapter 9: Godly Authority as It Applies to Parents

"Although it cannot be supposed that Eve . . ." is from *Biblical Commentary on the Old Testament*, by Karl Fredreich Keil and Franz Delitzsch, Hendrickson Publishers, 1996, Vol. I, page 108.

"We should (in my judgment) more correctly infer . . ." is from *Commentaries on the Book of Genesis* by John Calvin, Christian Classics Ethereal Library, 2009, Vol. I, page 191.

Chapter 10: The Role of Women in the Parental Process

"The devoted wife and mother finds her absorbing interest . . . " is from "Titus" in *The Expositor's Bible Commentary* by D. Edmond Hiebert, Frank E. Gaebelein, General Editor, Zondervan, 1978, Volume 11, pages 436-437.

"I can see in looking back that my first . . ." is from "The High Calling of Wife and Mother in Biblical Perspective" by Dorothy Patterson in the book *Recovering Biblical Manhood and Womanhood: A Response to Evangelical Feminism* by Wayne Grudem, Crossway, 2006, pages 364-365.

Chapter 11: Godly Authority as It Applies to the Godliness of Children

"I have used the phrase 'inherited sin' rather than . . .' " is from *Systematic Theology: An Introduction to Biblical Doctrine* by Wayne Grudem, Zondervan, 2009, page 494.

"In the forefront of the minds of Christian parents . . ." is cited from *A Theology of the Family*, Jeff Pollard and Scott Brown, editors, page 280.

"Let all of this be mixed with such love . . ." is from *A Theology of the Family*, Scott T. Brown and Jeff Pollard, editors, NCFIC Publishers, 2015, page 99.

Chapter 12: Godly Authority as It Applies to the Church

"It all started by Jesus calling a few men to follow Him . . ." is from *The Master Plan of Evangelism* by Robert E. Coleman, Revell, 2010, page 21.

"The New Testament also claims for the other apostles . . ." is from *The Gift of Prophecy* by Wayne Grudem, Crossway, 1988, page 28.

Chapter 13: Godly Authority as It Applies to the Eldership of the Church

"Jokes about the color of the carpet aside . . ." is from "Leadership Surveys Church Conflict," by Eric Reed, *Christianity Today*, 2004, and is available at http://www.christianitytoday.com/pastors/2004/fall/6.25.html

"These apostles had unique authority . . ." is from *The Gift of Prophecy* by Wayne Grudem, Crossway, 1988, page 276.

"It appears likely that there was no normative pattern . . ." is from *A Theology of the New Testament* by George Eldon Ladd, Wm. B. Eerdmans Publishing, 2010, page 103.

"Many build churches nowadays . . ." is from *Biblical Eldership* by Alexander Strauch, Lewis and Roth Publishers, 2016, page 67.

"Paul viewed the position . . ." is from *Elders and Leaders: God's Plan for Leading the Church—A Biblical, Historical, and Cultural Perspective* by Gene Getz, Moody Publishers, 2003, page 96.

Chapter 14: The Qualifications of an Elder

"That they did not differ at all . . ." is from *Thayer's Greek-English Lexicon*, Hendrickson Publishers, 1995, pages 535-536.

"A true desire to lead the family . . ." is from *Biblical Eldership* by Alexander Strauch, Lewis and Roth Publishers, 2016, page 83.

Chapter 15: The Gender of an Elder

"The leadership within a family is vested in the husband and father . . ." is from *Recovering Biblical Manhood and Womanhood: A Response to Evangelical Feminism* by Wayne Grudem, Crossway Books, 2006, pages 237-238.

"In the partnership of two spiritually equal human beings . . ." is from *Recovering Biblical Manhood and Womanhood,* by Wayne Grudem, Crossway Books, 2006, page 95 and pages 107-108.

"God is distinct from and transcendent . . ." is from *Evangelical Dictionary of Theology,* edited by Walter A. Elwell, Baker, 2001, page 455.

Chapter 16: Roles and Responsibilities for Women in the Church

" . . . most scholars detect a references to men and women in general . . ." is from *Women in the Church* by Andreas J. Kostenberger, Thomas R. Schreiner, and H. Scott Baldwin, editors, page 115.

"Paul does not forbid women . . ." is by Thomas R. Schreiner in *Recovering Biblical Manhood & Womanhood*, John Piper and Wayne Grudem, eds. Wheaton, Illinois: Crossway Books, 1991, page 132.

" . . . that women should learn . . ." is from *Women in the Church* by Andreas J. Kostenberger, Thomas R. Schreiner, and H. Scott Baldwin, editors, page 122.

"Women were to learn with entire submissiveness from the men . . ." is from *Women in the Church* by Andreas J. Kostenberger, Thomas R. Schreiner, and H. Scott Baldwin, editors, page 124.

"We think 1 Timothy 2:8-15 . . ." is from *Recovering Biblical Manhood & Womanhood*, John Piper and Wayne Grudem, eds. Wheaton, Illinois: Crossway Books, 1991, page 179.

"The proscription on women teaching men . . ." is from *Women in the Church* by Andreas J. Kostenberger, Thomas R. Schreiner, and H. Scott Baldwin, editors, page 134.

"This is the ground-meaning in actual usage . . ." is from *Grammar of the Greek New Testament in the Light of Historical Research* by A.T. Robertson, Amazon Digital Services, 2014, page 580.

Chapter 19: Some Final Thoughts

"Flew stated at the time that . . ." is from "My Pilgrimage from Atheism to Theism: An Exclusive Interview with Former British Atheist Professor Antony Flew," by Gary R. Habermas, *Biola News*, December 9, 2004.

"The concept of a 'pack' is ingrained in your dog's DNA . . ." is from *Cesar's Way: The Natural, Everyday Guide to Understanding and Correcting Common Dog Problems* by Cesar Millan, Crown Archetype, 2006.

"After a few days of Joanne and Anne setting up housekeeping . . ." is from *And the Word Came Power* by Joanne Shetler, Wycliffe, 2002.

ACKNOWLEDGEMENTS

To be part of the church of Jesus Christ is the greatest privilege of my life. This is because the Church is where I am connected to Him and His people. This relationship will last forever.

It is here I begin to acknowledge those who have contributed to my life and ministry and therefore to this book since *The Power of Submission* is really all about the Church. I am exceedingly thankful to God for the elders (too many to name) who have been on this journey of authority and submission with me. Their response to God's Word with me has been an immeasurable contribution to my thoughts and convictions concerning this critical subject.

Since this book is not primarily an academic achievement but rather an expression of a life experience with God, His Word, and His people, I thankfully and joyfully acknowledge the congregations, all in California, that have heard and received God's Word from me and responded with respect and submission to their elders. These include Calvary Union Church in Alhambra, Calvary Church of Placentia, Seacoast Community Church in Encinitas, Covina First Evangelical Free Church, the Chinese Congregation of the Calvary Community Church of Brea, and the Evangelical Free Church of Fullerton.

I am also grateful to God for Talbot Theological Seminary for grounding me in the complete trust in and submission to the infallible Word of God, the Bible. God's Word has been my source for everything I have taught or implemented in ministry. I have no other words to proclaim and live.

Completing this book could not have happened without the excellent work of my editor, Mike Yorkey. He provided an excellent balance between improving the text and protecting my narrative. This is not easily done, but he accomplished it with gracious professionalism and personal care for my message. Jessica Snell did an awesome job proofreading the manuscript.

I would be remiss if I didn't acknowledge the outstanding graphic design work of Emily Morelli. I gave her what I thought would be an impossible assignment for the front cover of depicting God's glory and majesty above, with all kinds of people below on the earth. She did an amazing work of depicting that concept in a way that touched my soul. I hope her book cover touches you as well. In addition, she designed the interior pages that invite you to read the text and hear its message.

I also appreciate a group of men who have encouraged me throughout the years. They have been an accountability and support team for my ministry and were instrumental in encouraging me to complete this book. They are Frank Sung, Mike Peters, John Coloumbe, Fred Ouderkerken, and Tiangang Qian. These are all godly men who are serving God and His church in their own locale.

Turning to family, I am exceedingly thankful for my four children—Lori Byrne, John C. Tebay, Kari Domene, and David Tebay—who trusted me enough and respected me enough to follow me through my own stumbling efforts of teaching them and effecting them concerning submission to authority, including my own and that of Grace, my wife. It was our great privilege to love them and seek to train them in God's ways. They have continued this teaching of God's ways with their own children, and they with their children. This is a gift of God's grace to us for all eternity.

Their gracious response to that training and looking to God beyond all that we ever were or did for them has been used of God to make them a blessing wherever they live and move in this world, and a glory to His name. They all continue to be an amazing source of encouragement in God's ways and truth for the both of us.

Lastly, and with the greatest thankfulness to God, I acknowledge the indispensable contribution of my wife, Grace, to my life and my ministry. She began ministering with me when we were teenagers. Her humble, sacrificial giving of herself throughout every ministry effort in which I was engaged in will only be completely valued in eternity.

I am aware that God gave me the "helper" who was most suited to my needs as we served Him together in the building of His church and the shepherding of His people of all ages.

This is why I dedicate this book to her—Grace Amabelle Tebay.

ABOUT THE AUTHOR

JOHN TEBAY did not want to be a preacher when he was growing up. He wanted to be a farmer, but two movements of God changed his mind. Most of the dairy herd on the farm he was preparing to enter as a junior partner died. In addition, the teaching of J. Vernon McGee at Biola College in 1949 was used by God to convince him that everything God did was perfect, and everything man did was a mess. He rationally, but enthusiastically, decided God would run his life, not himself.

He began to minister in music and youth at a small Baptist church in Pasadena, California, while in college. During his second year of seminary, he became the solo pastor of a small congregation in nearby Alhambra. After eight-and-a-half years, God moved him to Calvary Church of Placentia. It was here that he was taught, through God's Word, about eldership in the church as well as other crucial principles of church life and ministry. Forty-two years later, he resigned as Senior Pastor and subsequently became the Leadership Coach at Seacoast Community Church in Encinitas, California. Since then and currently, he serves as Pastor at Large wherever God opens the door.

Currently, he is the Leadership Coach of the Chinese Congregation of the Calvary Community Church of Brea. In addition, he consults, teaches, and encourages several other churches. His goal is to serve his Lord in the building and strengthening of His church as long as he has breath. His ministry has been enhanced by a Master of Divinity degree program at Talbot Theological Seminary and a Doctor of Ministry degree program at Fuller Theological Seminary. John has been married to his wife, Grace, for sixty-four years. They have four children, sixteen grandchildren, and a growing number of great-grandchildren— thirteen as of this writing. His family has been his first priority of ministry throughout their years together.

The Power of Submission is his first book, and he describe his motivation thusly:

> The reason I have written *The Power of Submission* is not because I have any ambition to become a published author, or for any expectation of financial reward. It is because I have a passion for God's people, the Church.
>
> I especially desire that pastors, elders, seminary professors, and students, as well as congregations, have a clear understanding of God's teaching in His Word about authority in the world, the family, and the church. The lack of clarity on this subject, in my experience, has brought division and disunity to governments, personal relationships, families, employees, employers, churches, and parachurch organizations.
>
> When authority is clear and godly as described in this book, there is unity, peace, and love that grows.

CONTACT JOHN TEBAY

If you or your church would like to contact John Tebay, please call or text him at (714) 504-5091. His email address is jandgtebay@yahoo.com.

Made in the USA
Middletown, DE
24 April 2019